SKYWARD

WHY FLYERS FLY

PHOTOGRAPHY & TEXT BY RUSSELL MUNSON

INTRODUCTION BY RICHARD BACH

(Overleaf, pages 2-3) Beechcraft G17S Staggerwing. The last version of the famous Model 17 series which began in 1932, the G17S was the most beautiful of all. Only 20 were assembled between 1946 and 1948. Surpassed in efficiency by other aircraft but never in elegance, the G17S was powered by a 450-h.p. Pratt & Whitney R-985 engine and carried four to five people in style at a maximum cruising speed of 174 knots (200 m.p.h.). NC 80305, shown here, is owned and flown by Staggerwing Club president Jim Gorman.

(Overleaf, pages 4-5) Canadair Challenger 601-3A. Built in Canada, the Challenger is the wide-body of corporate jets with a large passenger cabin and stand-up headroom. A typical interior configuration will coddle 10 passengers in easy chairs and a divan. A galley and lavatory—necessities considering the airplane's 3,600-nautical-mile range—are also provided. Two 8,650-pound-thrust GE fanjet engines push the Challenger up to a 41,000-foot ceiling and a normal cruise speed of 459 knots (528 m.p.h.).

(Overleaf, pages 6-7) The world as seen from an Eipper-Formance MX ultralight aircraft cruising along at 40 knots 1,000 feet above the North Carolina coast. Looking more like flying lawn chairs than airplanes, ultralights give the sensations of flight like no other machine.

(Overleaf, pages 8-9) Mooney 201. Capable, rugged, extremely efficient, and very popular, the four-place 201 will cruise at 169 knots (194 m.p.h.), burning a miserly 10.8 gallons of fuel per hour. It is powered by a 200-h.p. Lycoming engine.

(Overleaf, page 10) Cessna P210. General aviation's first practical, pressurized single-engine aircraft, the P210, or Pressurized Centurion, is powered by a 310-h.p. Continental engine that produces a cruising speed of 181 knots (208 m.p.h.) at 20,000 feet for four to six people.

This book is dedicated with love to my parents, Alberta and Russell Munson, Sr. Their support for whatever caught my interest, and tolerance for the aromas wafting up from the basement of darkroom chemicals, model-airplane engine exhaust, and smoke from homemade gunpowder as their son tested his rocket engines fashioned from .30-.30 shell casings deserves a medal for coolness under fire. Don't get me wrong; they weren't perfect. They never bought me a motorcycle.

—Russell Munson

I want to express my gratitude to FLYING magazine and all my colleagues there both past and present for whom much of the material in this book was originally conceived. Their help and friendship as we all explored our fascination of flight during the past 20-odd (I use the word advisedly) years has been an inspiration. Thank you all.

*I HAVE OFTEN SAID THAT
THE LURE OF FLYING
IS THE LURE OF BEAUTY...
THAT THE REASON FLYERS FLY,
WHETHER THEY KNOW IT OR NOT,
IS THE ESTHETIC APPEAL OF FLYING.*

—AMELIA EARHART

The crop duster, master of seat-of-the-pants flying. His life depends on it.

Designed by Marilyn F. Appleby.
Edited by Kathleen D. Valenzi, with the assistance of Heather A. Norton.
Photographs and text copyright © 1989 by Russell Munson. All rights reserved.
Introduction copyright © 1989 by Richard Bach. All rights reserved.
This book, or any portions thereof, may not be reproduced or transmitted
in any form or by any means, electronic or mechanical, including
photocopying, recording, or by any information storage and retrieval
system, without permission in writing from the publisher.
Photographs and text may not be reproduced without permission of Russell Munson.
Introduction may not be reproduced without permission of Richard Bach.
Library of Congress Catalog Card Number 89-84490
ISBN 0-943231-23-X
Opening quote excerpted from LAST FLIGHT by Amelia Earhart,
published 1937 by Harcourt, Brace and Co.
Printed and bound in Japan by Dai Nippon Printing Co., Ltd.
Published by Howell Press, Inc., 700 Harris Street, Suite B, Charlottesville, Virginia 22901. Telephone (804) 977-4006.
First Printing

HOWELL PRESS

CONTENTS

ADVENTURE   16

MY FRIEND THE CARPENTER   20

PAST PRESENT: BARNSTORMING ADVENTURES   25

WHY FLYERS FLY: JOHN COOK   40

GALLERY ONE   42

WHY FLYERS FLY: OLIVE BORGATTI   74

MEETING AN OLD FRIEND: LEARNING TO FLY THE DC-3   78

GALLERY TWO   86

TIME SUSPENDED: A DESERT REST HOME FOR AIRPLANES   112

WHY FLYERS FLY: JEFF MICHAEL   122

GALLERY THREE   124

WHY FLYERS FLY: NANCY BINK   142

RAPTURE OF THE HEIGHTS: AN ULTRALIGHT ADVENTURE   147

WHY FLYERS FLY: HENRY HAMPTON   154

GALLERY FOUR   156

WHY FLYERS FLY: ROBERT LOOMIS   170

CROSS-COUNTRY CUB: THE FREEDOM TO GO   175

GALLERY FIVE   196

APPENDIX: ABOUT AIR-TO-AIR PHOTOGRAPHY   206

ADVENTURE

(Left) The Beechcraft G17S Staggerwing's power plant, a Pratt & Whitney R-985. (Overleaf, pages 18-19) Stinson SM6000B Trimotor instrument panel.

On this day, Thursday, September 29, 1988, I am flying as a passenger on Piedmont Flight 1209 from Newark, New Jersey, to Jacksonville, Florida. It is 11:29 on a clear morning, and our Boeing 737 jet is only a third filled. Just now, on Cape Canaveral, the space shuttle Discovery is in its final countdown for launch. Though we are still far north of the Cape, our captain, Jim Azone, has promised to turn the airliner at the proper time so that we might be able to see some sign of the rocket.

At 11:38 Captain Azone announced, "They have liftoff." And a moment later, "Everything is normal." A cheer went up from my fellow passengers—men and women, young and old, all drawn together for the moment in wishing Discovery well.

"It's eight miles high," said Azone. "We can see it from the cockpit. I'm turning the plane westward now. Look for Discovery out the left side." All of the passengers except two moved to the left of the aircraft and squinted into the sun.

"Do you see it yet?" asked a gray-haired woman in the seat behind me.

"No. Yes, there it is." I pointed. In the distance a trail of smoke climbed up at a 45-degree angle, a line in the sky that marked the path of five astronauts in a remarkable machine lifting toward space to reclaim the sky two years after the sickening Challenger disaster. We were too far away to see the actual spacecraft from our 737, only the fading mark it left in the sky.

Yet, it was exciting for those of us watching aboard Flight 1209 to see even that and to be in the same sky at the same time. It captured our imaginations. Flight always has. It is a symbol for the spirit in each of us that seeks to be free of limitations. Flight is a symbol for adventure.

I know people who say that except for the exploration of space, there are no adventures left. They have all been done. So unless you have a powerful government to send you to astronaut school, this group argues, forget about big-time, page-one adventure. There are no opportunities left in today's world for an individual, acting alone and without great resources, to do such a thing. Lindbergh was the last, they say, and even he had outside backing, so forget about it. The argument of the Forget-It School seems logical if you ignore the dreary consequences of such thought.

Others believe that a life of adventure begins with a frame of mind that we choose. It is a way of looking at things, a matter of perspective. Followers of the Do-It School are convinced that life itself is an adventure, that making the front page is irrelevant in measuring the value of an experience, and that "It's already been done" is at best a poor excuse to stop living.

By now you may suspect where my sympathies lie. Perhaps almost everything has been done in one way or another, but everything hasn't been done in your way or mine. The fun is in doing it yourself, and thinking about it is the first step on that road. Adventure can take many forms and can be undertaken in different ways. One does not have to be Superperson, nor even able-bodied, to know the exhilarating freedom that it provides, for its home is inside of us. Some have the gift of being able to imagine something so vividly that it is almost as if they had physically lived the experience, very much like a dream from which we awake with senses full and reality for the moment in question. Most of us, though, find that participating in an activity is helpful in giving form to abstract notions. Short of being able to fly without the benefit of a machine, I know of no pursuit that comes closer to my concept of freedom and adventure than flying, especially in small, general aviation aircraft.

Sure, thousands have traveled across the country in a small plane. It's been done. But it is still an adventure for me each time, and I've been flying for half of my life. Every local hop is exhilarating. I love being in the air and seeing the world from such a unique perspective. It helps keep my priorities straight when things get pressing back on earth. Flying is never boring, I never get tired of it, and I never return from a flight without feeling grateful for the privilege of being up there.

It follows that I feel an affection and great respect for the machines that allow me to indulge my passion. Ennobled by their purpose, shaped by the wind, transformed from idea to reality by the genius of their designers and builders, aircraft, perhaps more than any other machine, cross the boundary between utilitarian devices and works of art.

One passion in a lifetime is a blessing. Two is good fortune beyond all expectation. Photography has been my second passion, again since childhood. Because I thought I had more to offer as a photographer than as a commercial pilot, I chose freelance photography as my profession. Yet, I couldn't imagine a life without flight, so I specialized in aerial photography.

Along the way, I have had experiences that were important to me and have met many wonderful people and airplanes. On these pages I would like to introduce you to some of them by putting you where I was so that my experience may be yours. Few of us may ever pilot a spacecraft, but most of the aircraft I am about to show you are flown everyday for business or pleasure by non-superhumans like you and me.

I believe that there is a desire in each of us— aviators and non-flyers alike—to see what lies beyond the next hill. That is the spirit of adventure, and flying is one way to seek it. SKYWARD is for those to whom the idea of flight is in some way an expression of themselves.

—Russell Munson

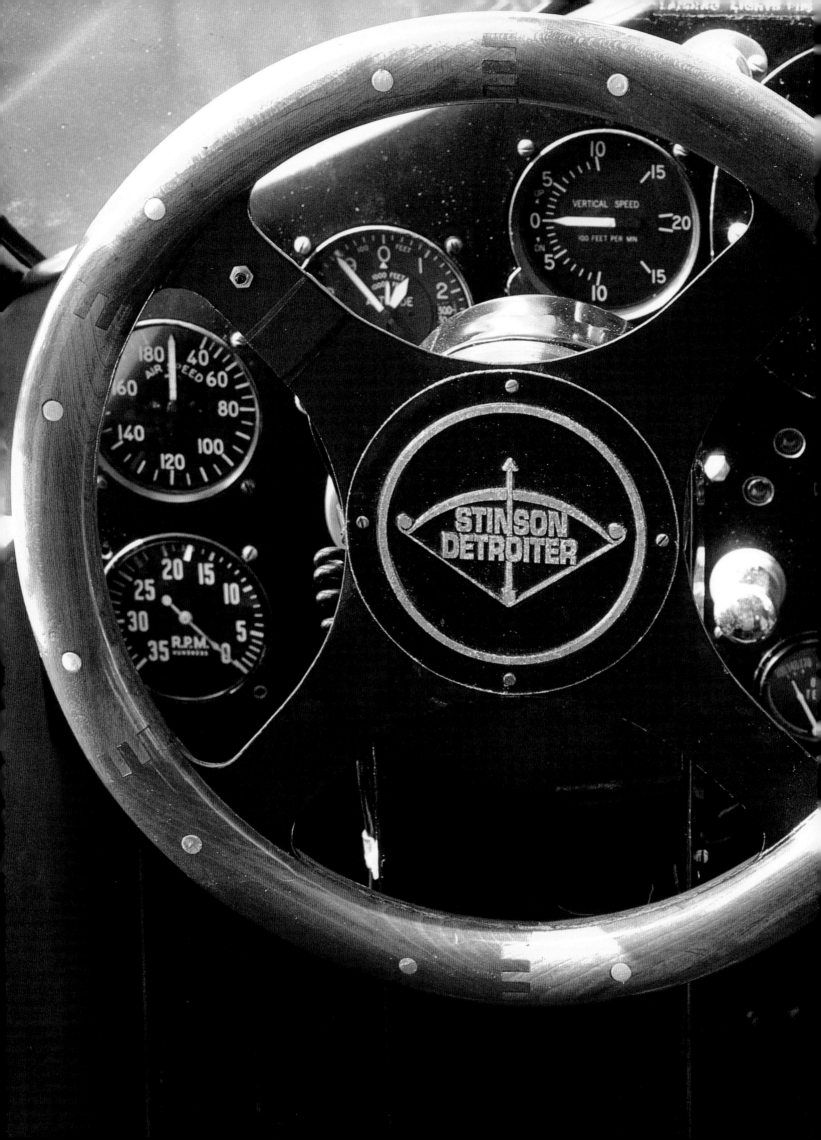

MY FRIEND THE CARPENTER

I've watched Russell Munson at work for 20 years, and I'm convinced at last that he's no photographer.

In real life, Munson is Captain Bruce Savage of Varney Speed Lines, arrived with night mail and passengers from Omaha and just this minute down from the cockpit of yonder Lockheed Vega.

Twentieth Century-Fox can cast anyone for a photographer, but to fill the role of Captain Savage they must have Russell Munson: tall as the better part of that Vega propeller, trace of a modest grin now for flying his ship safely through storms no bird would dare, 'membrance of a thousand tougher flights behind his eyes. Look at Munson, and you know that this fellow has been flying airplanes for a long while indeed.

Yet the man can change, as it suits him. When we were barnstorming together, town-to-town through the Midwest, he looked for all the world as though he were your next-door Kansas airplane pilot who'd brought his Kodak along for snapshots of the summer. It's easy to be yourself around Russell Munson, people found, because he's friendly and bright, straight and fair as Elm Street.

From the faces on the pages ahead, you can tell that Munson somehow turns his camera invisible—the people he meets come to trust him so they don't seem to notice there's a Nikon in his hand.

The only picture I remember him taking of me is one he wanted to make in flight, looking back across the biplane at vast Iowa below. To get that shot he had to unfasten his safety belt and stand up in the front seat, 2,000 feet over the cornfields. Now a man the size of Captain Savage, standing in the wind stream, shatters smooth air into fierce tornados over the rudder and elevators. I was not smiling in that picture because in all that buffeting the airplane was flying like half a ton of rock salt, and I was praying that the daredevil with the lens would please sit down.

After what I clocked as a lifetime's shooting, he finally slipped out of the wind and back into the cockpit. That's when I smiled at last. I don't remember noticing his camera for the rest of the tour.

When the summer was over, when Captain Savage had flown west with Varney Speed Lines and our barnstorming airplanes had fallen asleep in snow-blanket hangars, Russell Munson caught his subjects' dreams in a darkroom and set them in frames, on a studio wall.

When I looked into his landscapes of the summer, I knew that I had been right all along. My friend is no photographer; he is a mystical cosmic carpenter. What he makes with his camera, what he builds in magazines and books and art galleries around the world are not pictures but doorways, humming spaces he's carved loose from time and left open on all the pasts he's flown.

Each frame I saw changed from film into these eerie doors, through which float the lights and sounds, the colors and tastes of a different time. There aren't two dimensions here, but four. This minute, somehow, we can lean into his pictures and live what they are, hear alfalfa hay crunch underfoot, smell it mixed with Wright Whirlwind engine propeller blast, taste the knife-sound of flying-wires slicing the air into endless silver ribbons. Doorways, every one, each inviting us to drift through, if we wish, and become ourselves part of the living scene.

I'm a creature of one scene, I thought. Could it be that I'm a creature of them all? So long I stared back from page 83's cockpit window, watching passengers board, listening to murmurs and quiets, breathing thick Florida air, that I could move my hand without looking and feel airline throttles underneath. Drift through a different doorway, touch those massive cowl flaps, and we find there's engine oil on our fingers, and the lingering cold of shaped aluminum.

Some might say that the only people who can slip down Munson's passageways are the ones who have been there already; that if we haven't flown, we can't begin to see these images in any more dimensions than two.

I don't think so. Every flyer I've known has nourished two qualities before ever they earned a pilot's license: they care about beauty and they are romantics, every one.

SKYWARD is a book for every curious romantic, flyer or not, who looks to the sky and wonders what it's like to be someone who calls that place home. Turn the page, and welcome to the beauty-filled world of Captain Bruce Savage and of his carpenter friend, Russell Munson.

—Richard Bach

(Above and facing) A barnstorming Travel Air 4000.

PAST PRESENT:

BARNSTORMING

ADVENTURES

In the years following World War I, a new way to live, or sometimes starve, became possible for anyone with a few hundred dollars and a wish to fly. Surplus government airplanes, mostly Curtiss Jenny and Standard J1 trainers, were being sold at give-away prices. Many were brand new, still sealed unassembled in factory crates; others were so thoroughly used, it was difficult to distinguish the crate from the airplane. All were there for the taking at designated depots around the country.

Customers ranged from seasoned, ex-Army pilots to bold, young adventurers with more enthusiasm than flying experience. Of course, none was required. Pilot licenses had not yet caught on. Just buy it and fly it, folks. To their credit, most people didn't fly off without a few hours of instruction. There were some, though, with more self-confidence than common sense, who simply bought a ship and taught themselves to fly by taxiing faster and faster, then making little crow hops into the air, and finally longer ones until they were flying for real. For onlookers it was an entertaining process of elimination to see who had the right stuff. Fortunately, it is hard to kill yourself at 45 miles per hour, and the frequently needed replacement parts were plentiful and cheap.

Experienced or not, these pilots and their clattering biplanes were soon landing in farmers'

fields everywhere, taking paying passengers for rides and giving lessons to anyone with cash. A new, free-hand lifestyle of adventure, risk, and beauty was born from desire and economic opportunity. With it, the promise of aviation was spread across the land like seed upon the wind.

To most people back then, the mere sight of an airplane flying overhead was noteworthy, but to have one piloted by a begoggled, godlike creature in a leather jacket swoop down and land in your own town, well now, that was cause for excitement. And where there is excitement, there is money to be made.

Your average adventuresome pilot with a bedroll and a beat-up biplane could do all right hopping the locals at a few bucks a head, at least for a while. In the good times it was even possible to put a little money aside for an overhaul or trade up to a newer machine, such as the coveted Waco, Eaglerock, or Travelair biplanes. When the crowds dwindled after a couple of days in one place, the helmeted hero threw his gear into the passenger cockpit, tossed a wave to the always present star-struck-kid-with-dog, and gunned his engine in search of the next town that said hello.

With few flying jobs available, military or civilian, the life of an itinerant pilot was the most accessible way of getting into aviation. Living out of their hip pockets, surviving by their wits,

25

they operated either alone, or in small bands, with wing-walkers and parachutists as added attractions. These flying gypsies, who came to be known as barnstormers, were aviation's follow-on to the romantic sky heroes of World War I. They prowled the prairies and farmlands of America well into the 1930s, but by then their ranks had thinned to a handful of flying circuses. The lone barnstormer had become extinct, the victim of economics and the rigors of transience.

Of those who stayed in flying, most were absorbed into the more stable opportunities of the then rapidly growing aviation industry. Some went with the airlines; others, gypsies at heart who preferred their adventures raw, flew in the desolate reaches of the world where air transport was still free of the advancing regulation back home; many settled down along the way at one of their barnstorming stops that just felt like home. In contrast to their previous way of life, the latter were called fixed-base operators, or FBOs as they are known today, and sold airplanes, fuel, maintenance, flying lessons, and charter flights. They formed the essential service backbone upon which private and corporate aviation grew.

By the time I bought my own plane (a used Piper Super Cub) in 1967, barnstormers were nothing more than dashing characters in history books. Like the old biplanes, Cubs are great airplanes for boondock flying, but you can't move back the clock. Closing my eyes and imagining what it must have been like was the nearest my plane and I would ever come to living the life of a gypsy pilot, I thought. The world had changed drastically in 40 years. Modern-day barnstorming would surely be impossible in a time of lawsuits and more insurance policies per capita than jars of peanut butter. It was my good fortune that a friend proved otherwise.

To author/pilot Richard Bach, impossible has

The barnstormer's billboard.

Rio, Wisconsin.

The CANDO method of navigation in progress. Clockwise from left: Steve Young, Stu McPherson, Jack Brown, Chris Cagle, Glen Norman, and Richard Bach.

no meaning. Barnstorming does. By reading about the period and talking to old-timers who had flown in the 1920s and 1930s, Richard learned how they lived back then, what they looked for when picking a field to operate out of, what size towns were best, and how to let the residents of an area know you were there. Would it be possible, he wondered, to live as a gypsy pilot in the world of now? With the help of his 1929 Parks P2-A biplane, and later a 1929 Travelair 4000, he found out. I flew on two barnstorming trips (along with others of Richard's flying buddies) —one in the summer of 1968, and again five years later.

As The Great American Flying Circus, our ships ranged from the Parks and Travelair biplanes of the barnstorming period to Aeronca, Cub, and Luscombe monoplanes designed in the late 1930s. Numbering from two to as many

as six airplanes, our group included at various times an airline pilot, a flight-school owner and former barnstormer, a dentist, a flight instructor, a farmer, a student who liked to parachute jump, two writers, and a photographer. Richard's fascinating experiment, our mutual love of flying, and everyone's curiosity and drive to live for a while as barnstormers brought us from all over the country to fly together in the farmlands of mid-America.

Each day we chose a flight leader and, once airborne, the rest would follow him to a destination usually not known even by the leader until we got there. Some days we headed whichever way the wind was blowing in order to save gas; other times, to a town we'd liked on a previous trip. But the most interesting method of setting a course was employing what might best be called the Crawling Ant Navigational Decision Option, or CANDO. This is a rarely used but highly arbitrary formula, particularly suited to deadbeats like us.

The CANDO method worked like this. Richard would spread a map on the ground and place an ant (ants always seemed to be available when we needed them) on the spot where we were. As the ant crawled, Richard would follow its path with a felt-tipped pen, marking our course on the chart. With that done, we had a thorough pilot briefing:

"Who wants to be flight leader today?" No response.

"Okay, Stu, you be the leader."

"I was leader yesterday."

"Okay, Spense, you be leader. Do you have any idea where we're going?"

"No."

"Okay, let's get going."

We'd climb in our planes, take off, and form up into a dangling, rag-tag formation, following our leader in search of the first likely town.

To be suitable for barnstorming stops, a town had to meet several qualifications. First, it had to be small. A population under 1,000 was preferable. Big towns were too sophisticated to be interested in us or we in them. Second, we preferred a place with no airport so that the appearance of our airplanes was an unusual event. Next, there had to be a field on an accessible road within walking distance of town that was fairly smooth, clear of obstructions, and long enough to operate from comfortably. The area surrounding the chosen field had to be open so that an uneventful emergency landing could be made should one of our engines fail at any point while flying passengers. Each of us had an intimate knowledge of our own and our machine's limitations, which we did not exceed. That was our best insurance policy.

Despite rather rigid requirements, finding a good spot usually didn't take more than an hour or two. Most often it was a recently harvested farm field. We landed, got the owner's permission to use his property, then tacked up Richard's "Fly $3 Fly" sign on the fence near the road. Thundering off again, we circled town, performing various maneuvers to attract attention. At the moment we supposed the townspeople's excitement was near the bursting point, all aircraft sped back over the chosen field, where we dropped our intrepid parachutist as the finale, spiraling around him as he floated to the ground. If we had planned correctly in picking the proper time and place, people were already rushing up when our jumper landed to see if he was okay. Seizing the moment, he quickly pulled a roll of tickets out of his jump suit and began selling airplane rides as the rest of us taxied up.

Other times, no one showed up at all for a while, especially if we landed on a weekday during working hours. But from Richard's research, later chronicled in his book NOTHING BY CHANCE, we knew that if we sat under the wing in the shade, chewing on grass stems kind of like we didn't care, someone would arrive.

A barnstormer's motel.

"See your town from the air, folks." Passengers get an aerial view of their home from the front seat of a Travel Air 4000.

They always did. The first was either an out-of-breath kid racing up on his bicycle or a concerned farmer in a pickup truck asking if we needed help. In either case, word of what we were doing spread quickly through town, and by evening the dirt road bordering the field would be lined with pickups, cars, and bicycles.

"Are these old things safe?" someone would ask.

"Of course. How do you think they got to be so old?" one of us would answer.

After the first brave soul bought a ride and returned, face all smiles, to tell his friends how his farm looked from the air, it was like a dam broke. From then until the late summer sunset, we hopped passengers and swapped stories with the people we met, learning about their lives and telling them about ours.

Sitting in their cars with the doors open,

leaning against a truck fender, or sprawled on a picnic blanket eating fried chicken and potato salad, these gentle people watched our airplanes go and come from 10-minute rides carrying their neighbors and family members. Some of our passengers had never been in the air before. For a day or two our lives overlapped because of an idea and a few old airplanes.

The mornings were for housekeeping: attending to the airplanes' needs, buying groceries, doing our meager laundry, and using the local gas station for other of life's necessities.

Our simple engines ran fine on auto gas. In rural areas fuel dealers have tank trucks to deliver to the farms. They were always happy to swing by our field. We did use aviation oil, however, and one of us would fly to the nearest airport to pick up a case whenever we needed it.

In the evening, passengers gone home, we

Townspeople await their turn.

31

buttoned up the airplanes and divided the day's profits. At $3.00 per passenger, accepted as a donation, we always made enough for hamburgers and gasoline. For dinner we either cooked over a campfire or walked into town for burgers and shakes. Later, back at the field, we sat for a while on the ground, talking and swatting mosquitoes, maybe resting against the wheel of an airplane with its dark silhouette above us formed by a star-filled sky. We talked about the day's adventures and the people we had flown; we talked about other flights in other airplanes; and we talked about the lives we had left to come do this. When the yawns outnumbered the words, each neobarnstormer unrolled his sleeping bag under a wing, carefully placing it so the dew wouldn't drip from the trailing edge onto his face in the morning, and slept until first light. We were in a different place, in a different time, living in harmony with its own rhythm.

The readjustment coming back was never easy, and never more so than from my last barnstorming trip. I took off in the Super Cub from Rio, Wisconsin, on a cloudy afternoon, not being able to prolong my departure for New York any longer. Rio, pronounced Rye-O, is a charming town of some 800 good-hearted people, who had turned our final stop into a five-day feast. A front was moving in from the west, and the weather had already turned sullen, so I thought it best to get as far as I could before it socked in. Most of our group had left earlier to return to their previous lives. Those who remained took local hops with each other for fun, watched the sky grow more obscured, ate a sandwich, talked about the summer, and tried to pretend for a while longer that its end had not come.

Onlooker in Rio, Wisconsin.

(Above) Passenger in
Kahoka, Missouri.
(Left) Another passenger
showing a snapshot of an
airplane he built during
the real barnstorming days.

I flew on in deteriorating weather with my thoughts revisiting all the towns we had barnstormed: Ferris and Pecatonica, Illinois; Kahoka, Albany, Maryville, Queen City, Taylor and Osgood, Missouri; Albia, Mt. Ayr, Hedrick, Amana, and Clarinda, Iowa; Horton, Onaga, Washington, Frankfort, and Seneca, Kansas; Cook, Nebraska; and, of course, Rio. I saw the smiling faces of the lean, weathered old man and his granddaughter in the front cockpit of the Parks in Seneca; smelled the freshly mowed hay and toasted marshmallows in Ferris; and remembered looking to either side out of the opened windows of my Cub at the brightly colored airplanes of my friends, bobbing and floating freely 500 feet above the broad landscape of the Midwest, not knowing nor caring exactly where we would rest that night.

All I could see now from my cockpit was land in shades of gray that faded into a monochromatic veil. Visibility was down to a mile and the ceiling at 500 feet, not enough for comfortable visual flight. I looked at an aeronautical chart for the first time in weeks and followed the Rock River to the Janesville, Wisconsin, airport. It started to rain as I finished tying down the Cub, and I caught a ride from the FBO's office to the nearest motel. My room was a small square, institutionally colored, with a bed, table, and chair. Instead of fresh-mowed hay, it smelled of stale cigarettes masked by pine spray. The window, television, and mirror were arranged in a row like three surreal looking glasses. One was storm gray, one was blank, and one showed me in an alien place. For the last 20 nights, I had slept on the ground and flown every day. My flight from Rio had taken only 45 minutes, but I had traveled 50 years too quickly. The time-warp bends set in.

But the weather delay provided time to adjust to the disorientation of reentry, to savor the life of the barnstormer, and to remember what someone had once told me in my sleep: either you make your life what you want it to be, or others will make it what they think it should be.

If you should ever wonder whether it would be possible to wing off on a barnstorming trip today, right now, in a time when each sneeze brings a lawsuit, when greed is god, and it is sometimes hard to remember what open spaces and open people are like; if you should ever wonder, please know that the integrity of hayfields and the sky don't change, nor the character of those who live in their midst. At heart, both are the same today as they were when the first barnstormer climbed down from his ship and said, "See your town from the air, folks. Three dollars a ride."

Barnstormer Richard Bach.

A 1929 Parks.

(Clockwise from top) Passengers, a passenger's waiting husband, and future passengers at a Great American Flying Circus barnstorming stop.

(Above) Leaving is one of the bittersweet facts of the barnstormer's life.
(Overleaf, pages 38-39) Travel Air 4000.

(Above) Captain John Cook and the Concorde. (Overleaf, pages 42-43) Falconjet 50. Magnificent travel for 8 to 12 corporate passengers, the Falcon 50 is powered by three Garrett turbofan engines of 3,700-pounds thrust each, and it has a maximum cruise speed of 475 knots (546 m.p.h.) and ceiling of 49,000 feet. With eight passengers, it can take off from a 4,700-foot runway and fly 3,500 nautical miles with IFR fuel reserves.

JOHN COOK

I was in London throughout World War II as a young kid, so I used to see all the battles going on in the air and all the wrecks on the ground as well. The Royal Air Force fighter pilots were heroes. Much later, when I finished school, I decided to join the Air Force.

After soloing a Tiger Moth at Cranwell, I was shipped to Rhodesia, one of the most beautiful countries I have ever seen, for further training in Chipmunks and Harvards. From the air we saw hippos, ostriches, and other wildlife. I can still smell Rhodesia when I think about it, the wonderful smell of the earth.

My class came back to England very proud of our new wings, and we went on to jets. I was sent up to Worksop in the Midlands for training in all-weather fighters. I remember getting off at the railroad station nearby the base on a lovely, clear day and hearing a loud whine. I looked up and saw a Gloster Meteor over the rooftops. She had just taken off. The gear was coming in, and she went right on up into a half loop and did a roll off the top. Two weeks later I was doing it too.

I enjoyed my service flying very much. That is where I learned the discipline of flying. In order to have the freedom of flight you must have the discipline. Discipline prevents crashes.

By 1956 the services were cutting down on personnel. I had chums who were with British Overseas Airways, the forerunner of British Air, and they seemed to be enjoying themselves, so I decided to have a go at that.

I spent my first three years on the airline flying all over Africa and the Far East as a navigator in Argonauts. It was a marvelous machine, but having to fly as a navigator was very frustrating. I moved to the DeHavilland Comet IV on the North Atlantic route in 1959, first as navigator, then as copilot, flying with some magnificent chaps. Those were still the early days of jet flying across the Atlantic, and to us the Comet IV was the Queen of the skies, a beautiful aircraft to fly and to look at. But on descents after coming across the ocean, we had to wear our raincoats, because all of the condensation that had accumulated in the cockpit came trickling down on us.

In 1964 I moved up to the Vickers VC-10, first as copilot, then as captain in 1970. I moved over to the Boeing 747 in 1973 as a training captain. Unlike in the United States, all of our training captains must also be line captains. In other words, part of your time is spent flying the routes as a regular line captain, and part is spent training people.

In 1976 I moved to the Concorde program in the same capacities. She is a fantastic airplane and, again, a beautiful-looking aircraft. That delta wing design, which will take you through the speed of sound without the passengers feeling so much as a ripple, is amazing.

My first takeoff in the Concorde in 1977 will always stick in my mind. Nothing in my previous flying experience gave the slightest clue of what it would be like. With a weight of only 115 tons and 38,000 pounds of thrust from each of four engines, the acceleration is tremendous. Light the afterburners, and you're off like a rocket. And of course, the performance numbers are much higher than those for a conventional airliner. We start our cruise at 50,000 feet, then as fuel burns off making us lighter, we cruise-climb to 60,000. Our cruising speed is Mach 2, twice the speed of sound. That is equivalent to one mile every 2¾ seconds, or 23 miles per minute.

To fly the Concorde one must really love flying, because she is a demanding airplane. Not difficult, but different. We expect our pilots to maintain a given angle of attack to a ¼-degree tolerance, and when we say fly the downwind leg at 250 knots, we don't mean 249 or 251.

The delta wing has different lift characteristics than a conventional wing. At high angles of attack, such as on takeoff and landing approaches, the slightest change of attitude causes very large changes in drag and, consequently, in power requirements. The Canarsie approach at Kennedy Airport is a good example where all of these factors come into play. The approach is a visual one delineated by flashing strobe lights on the ground that mark a curving, descending path to the runway. So there you are, nose up 11 degrees, the airplane's beak tilted down so you can see, and you can feel in the controls a hammering from the large vortex generated by delta wings at high angles of attack. There is quite a bit of vibration and noise in the cockpit. It is touch, touch, touch all the way down, keeping her exactly on balance. The pilot must have a good set of hands to do it right.

On the Atlantic route you are most often over cloud, but on the Bahrain-London trip, the weather is usually clear starting out, and the view is fantastic. From 60,000 feet you can see the curvature of the earth. Over the Red Sea you can look at the Gulf of Aqaba to the north and down the Nile Valley to Luxor in the south. You can see for 350 miles. Once past Crete and passing the boot of Italy, the passengers get an idea of the tremendous speed from seeing how quickly known landmarks go by.

Concorde gives you a perspective that is really quite mind-boggling. It makes you realize what the astronauts saw and had such a hard time describing.

I fly because I love flying. I don't really care what the machine is. Obviously, Concorde is the ultimate, but I love flying anything.

—*John Cook, Captain,*
British Air Concorde, Fleet, England

(Above) Landing at Stapleton Field, Denver, Colorado, as seen from the cockpit of a deHavilland of Canada DHC-7. (Facing) Boeing 727s at Washington National Airport.

(Above) Mitsubishi Diamond 1A. Designed in Japan and assembled in the United States, the Diamond 1A carries seven passengers at 420 knots (483 m.p.h.). Beechcraft of Wichita bought Mitsubishi's corporate-jet design, and an improved version called the Beechjet is now built in the United States. (Facing) Night takeoff of a Boeing 727 at Kennedy Airport.

(Above) Falcon 200 cabin. (Left)
Speed brakes, which can be extended
to quickly slow the Falcon or allow
it to descend rapidly without building
up excessive airspeed. (Facing)
Falconjet 200. Built by Dassault
in France and outfitted with in-
teriors and avionics by the Falconjet
Corporation in the United States,
Falcons are considered by their
owners to be the Mercedes Benz of
business jets. The 200 is the mid-
size model, which typically carries
six to nine passengers at a normal
cruise speed of 471 knots (542
m.p.h.). Certified ceiling for the jet
is 42,000 feet; two Garrett AFT3
engines of 5,200-pounds thrust get
the job done.

(Above and facing) Piaggio P.180 Avanti. A bold new design in the corporate turboprop market by the venerable Italian aircraft manufacturer, the Avanti is startling both in appearance and performance. Powered by two pusher-prop Pratt & Whitney PT-6 800-s.h.p. engines, the Avanti was meticulously designed for a 400-knot (460-m.p.h.) cruise speed with low fuel consumption but without sacrificing the advantages of a large, five-to-nine-place passenger cabin. Prototype Number 2, pictured here, proves the ambitious performance projections to be on target. (Overleaf, pages 52-53) Piper Cheyenne 400 LS. With two 1,000-s.h.p. Garrett turboprops and huge four-blade Dowty-Rotol props, the 400 LS has a normal cruise of 334 knots (384 m.p.h.) and a ceiling of 41,000 feet for six to nine passengers.

(Above) TBM 700 Prototype. A joint venture between Aerospatiale/Socata of France, Valmet of Finland, and Mooney of the United States, the TBM 700 is a slick single-engine turboprop that promises to carry six to eight people at a cruising speed of 300 knots (345 m.p.h.). It has a maximum ceiling of 30,000 feet for a maximum range of 2,000 nautical miles. Powered by a Pratt & Whitney 700-s.h.p. PT-6 engine, the TBM 700 could open a new chapter in corporate aviation. If advance orders and the performance and beauty of this prototype are any indication, the TBM 700 is well on its way to creating a new market: the single-engine turboprop business plane. (Facing) Piper Cheyenne III just before touchdown. (Overleaf, pages 56-57) Piper Malibu. One of the most significant single-engine airplanes since the Beech Bonanza, the Malibu began on a clean sheet of paper rather than as an evolution of an existing aircraft. Designed primarily by Jim Griswald, the Malibu is a pressurized, six-place, air-conditioned cabin-class that cruises at 215 knots (247 m.p.h.) at 25,000 feet powered by a 310-h.p. Continental TSIO-520 engine.

Air and Space 18-A. This two-place autogiro is powered by a 180-h.p. Lycoming engine turning a pusher prop mounted behind the cabin; it cruises at 65 knots (75 m.p.h.). Autogiros provide near-helicopter performance at a much lower cost. Unlike a helicopter's, an autogiro's rotor is not connected to the engine in flight. It turns like a windmill from the pressure of the air as the craft is propelled through the sky by a conventional airplane propeller. Takeoff and landing rolls are very short, but autogiros cannot duplicate a helicopter's vertical takeoff and landing capabilities.

Cessna 182 Skylane. One of the most popular planes ever, the 182 is comfortable, easy to fly, simple to maintain, and reasonably fast. Powered by a 230-h.p. Continental engine, the 182 carries four people at a cruising speed of 142 knots (163 m.p.h.).

(Above) The beautifully designed and equipped cockpit of the British Aerospace 800 corporate jet. (Right) A TBM 700. (Facing) Gulfstream Aerospace Perigrine. The Perigrine was one of those visionary airplanes that never made it past the prototype, which flew in 1983. Designed to be an owner-flown, single-engine, 331-knot (381-m.p.h.) personal jet, the Perigrine was to carry six people at 35,000 feet for a $1.6-million price tag. Despite an enthusiastic advertising campaign, not enough orders were received to justify production of Gulfstream president Allen Paulson's pet project. (Overleaf, pages 62-63) Mitsubishi Diamond 1A.

(Clockwise from upper left) The Polish Pezetel PZL-104 Wilga, Piaggio P.180 Avanti, Cessna 206 on Edo amphibious floats, and Mooney 201.

(Clockwise from upper left) Cessna 340, Gulfstream American Perigrine prototype, Beechcraft V35B Bonanza, and Allison turboprop-powered Beechcraft A-36 Bonanza. (Overleaf, pages 66-67) Allison A-36 Bonanza. With its normal Continental 300-h.p. piston engine replaced by an Allison 420-s.h.p. turbo-prop, the Beechcraft A-36 climbs at 1,900 feet per minute and cruises at 208 knots (239 m.p.h.). Allison's conversion is not inexpensive, but the improvements in performance, smoothness, and lowered noise level are impressive. (Overleaf, pages 68-69) Pezetel PZL-104 Wilga. Built in Poland and sold worldwide, the Wilga is a four-place, 82-knot (94-m.p.h.) bush plane designed to do donkey labor out of improved airstrips.

(Below) Cessna 310. One of the early light twins, the 310 became an instant hit in 1954 and remained in production for 27 years. This 310 II is powered by 260-h.p. Continental engines and cruises at 192 knots (221 m.p.h.) carrying four to six people. (Facing) Beechcraft V35B Bonanza. The classic V-tailed Bonanza first flew in 1945 and began production in 1947. Ralph Harmon's design instantly became the benchmark by which all high-performance, single-engine aircraft were measured throughout the V35's 38-year production run. For most of that time it was unsurpassed in speed, comfort, and handling—a pilot's airplane. The last model, the V35B, was powered by a 285-h.p. Continental engine and carried four at 172 knots (198 m.p.h.). (Overleaf, pages 72-73) Falcon 100. The smallest Falcon model is big on performance, cruising at 492 knots (566 m.p.h.) with four to eight passengers. It is powered by two 3,230-pound-thrust Garrett turbofan jets.

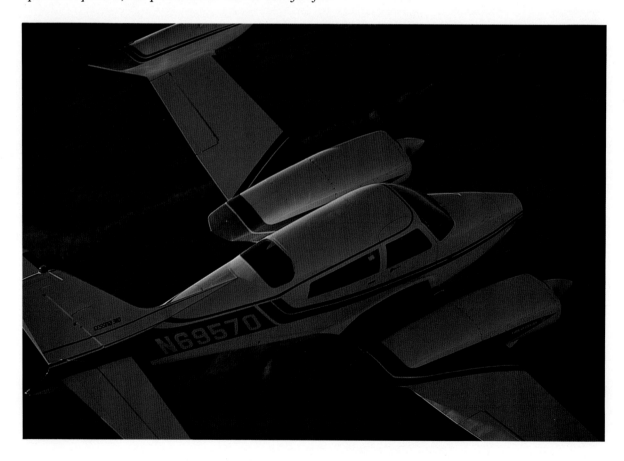

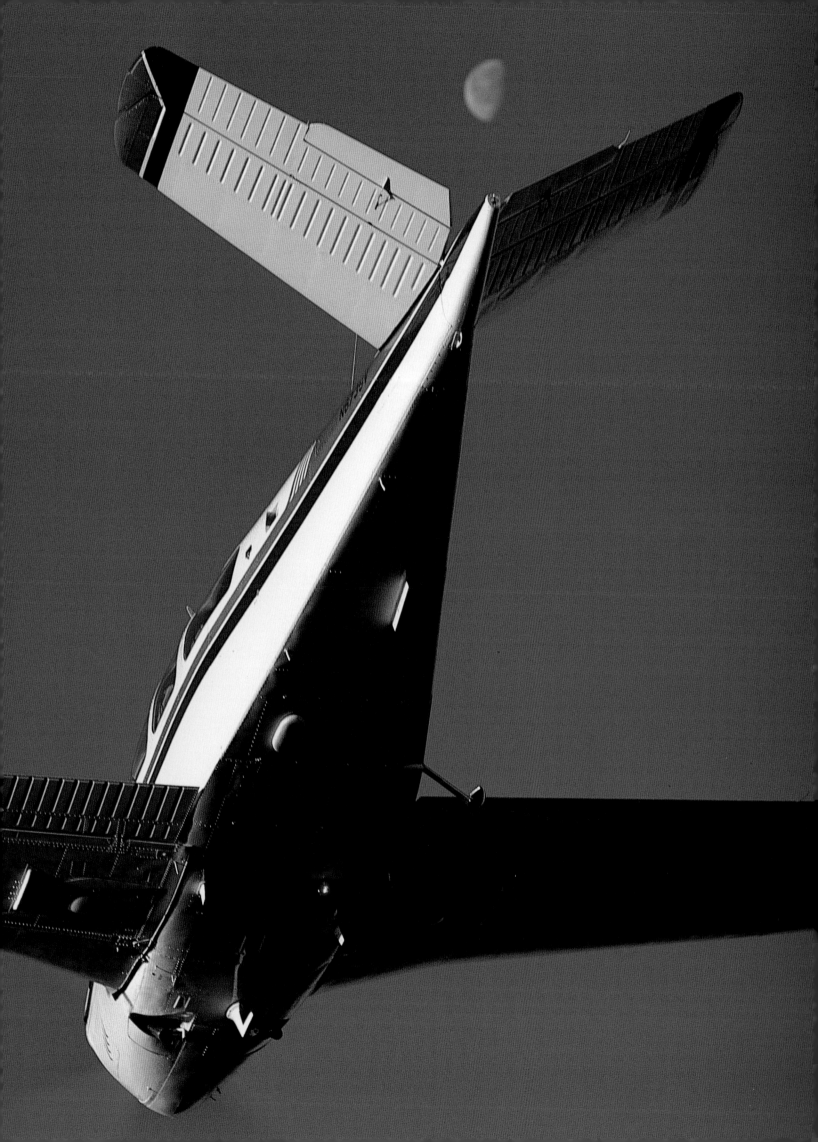

(Above) Olive Borgatti in the cockpit of her Cessna Citation jet. (Overleaf, pages 76-77) Douglas DC-3. If one airplane were to be chosen as the greatest ever built, the DC-3 would win hands down. More than any other aircraft, it introduced air travel to the world. This particular DC-3, N310K, was flying daily as a freighter when it was adorned with American Airlines livery to grace the pages of FLYING magazine's 50th-anniversary issue. American Airlines put their first DC-3 on the line in 1936.

OLIVE BORGATTI

I had never had any particular interest in flying as a child, and as an adult, had only flown on airliners until 1967. That year, my husband and I took a trip to Australia. We wanted to visit the Outback, but the only way to get there was in a small plane. Now in the previous 20 years, I had flown practically all over the world in airliners, and to me small planes were something you just didn't fly in. But I really wanted to see the interior of Australia, so we took a small plane. It turned out to be fantastic, really a delight. You could see everything, and the pilot landed on these little dirt strips on ranches to deliver packages along the way. It was such a delightful flight that I figured, "This is for me. I'm going to take up flying."

As soon as I got back, I started ground school at Worcester Airport. My husband, son-in-law, and a friend went with me. Later, I bought a second-hand Cessna 182, which is a fun plane, and learned to fly in it. At first I thought about discontinuing the lessons because my husband Spag was prone to airsickness. He had to take motion-sickness pills even on commercial airliners, and I thought, "What's the use of going on when he won't be able to fly with me." But he actually made me a better pilot, because I learned to fly very smoothly so that he would be comfortable. He never takes a pill at all now.

With my schedule at the company and juggling that to fit the instructor's schedule, plus weather delays, it took me just over a year to get my private pilot license. But I got it in November 1972. I was fifty-four years old.

Learning to fly was very exciting. I had never realized how many lakes there were in New England. You'd see the green trees and bright blue water, and it was just beautiful. I really enjoyed that. At that time I was thinking of flying only for pleasure rather than using it in the business.

Later, we could see that it might be handy to have a company plane that we could go to trade shows in and take some of our employees with us as we always do. So in 1974 we bought a twin-engined airplane, a Rockwell Commander Shrike. I already had my instrument rating by then, and I added a multi-engine rating and got my commercial license after buying the Shrike. The Shrike was a wonderful airplane, but after 10 years, we wanted something faster, so we bought a Turboprop Commander. I went to Oklahoma City where the airplane was built to learn to fly it at the Flight Safety Corporation's training facility there.

In 1987 we bought a jet, the Cessna Citation II, a very comfortable airplane. It flies like a dream, and it fits me. I'm 4 feet 11 inches tall, and Peter Woiciechowski, the head of our flight department, is 6 feet 5, and we're both comfortable in the cockpit. I went to the Flight Safety School in Wichita to get the Citation type-rating. As you may know, the FAA requires pilots of all jet aircraft, or any other aircraft with a maximum gross weight of more than 12,500 pounds, to have a type-rating in the specific aircraft they fly. The Flight Safety training was very intensive and thorough. Almost all jets require a crew of two, so Peter and I both have type-ratings and trade off flying from the left seat.

In high-flying airplanes like turboprops and jets, you certainly don't see the ground as much as you do from a 182, but I've seen some beautiful skies. Just beautiful. It is a whole different world.

We use the airplane strictly for transportation now. For example, this last Thursday, I went to Atlanta, and the next day I went to Vero Beach and back to Atlanta, then the next day to Worcester, then twice to New York the day after. It is great to fly like that, and it really keeps your skills sharp.

The Citation is great, because it is easy to handle. I just love it. Business trips are a lot more fun when you do the flying yourself. Since I spend so much time in the office listening to problems, I find it relaxing to fly. In the airplane there are no telephones ringing, nobody to bother me. I can do what I want to do, and I am busy in a pleasant way that I enjoy—far removed from office business. It is good for me.

One of the most beautiful sights I have seen was one night coming back from Chicago in the Turbo Commander. We saw the northern lights, and it was magnificent, a beautiful display of color. The whole sky was lit up with a line of sparkling lights of all different hues.

I am seventy-one now and, fortunately, in good health. I will fly for as long as I can pass the medical. When I can't, I'll say, "Well, I really enjoyed it." My only regret is that I didn't start flying sooner.

—Olive Borgatti, Corporation President,
Shrewsbury, Massachusetts

MEETING AN OLD FRIEND:
LEARNING TO FLY THE DC-3

Towering clouds were all that lay between Chicago and Cleveland that night, still the roughest, wettest, and most violently beautiful I have ever seen. They surrounded us, these restless, flexing, gray-green-black creatures of unknowable power, flashing like artillery batteries. No matter how close I pressed my little face to the window, their tops remained beyond sight, beyond even a child's imagination.

How dare we mere humans trespass their sky in this metal mosquito? They enveloped our machine, firing us upward like popcorn, suspending our bodies weightless and breathless for a timeless moment, then dropping us like a 25,000-pound boulder. That must be what they call an air pocket, I thought, as we entered the next updraft in a spine-crushing reversal that brought the hearts and stomachs of most of my fellow passengers to their mouths.

But I was too thrilled to be sick, too ignorant to be scared, and so captivated by the idea of flight that I passed the whole trip with my face to the plexiglass looking at a place I had never been. Sometimes I could see only my own reflection and the green glow of the wing-tip navigation light in the mist that swept past my window. The light would flicker and fade as it passed in and out of thick cloud. Beyond it lay the unknown, the beauty, excitement, and adventure of being in the air. Beyond it, also, lay my future.

The occasion for this trip was a father-son outing for United Air Lines' employees to see the 1948 Cleveland Air Races. We flew from Chicago to Cleveland aboard United Airlines President "Pat" Patterson's DC-3—the Mainliner O'Connor—which was beautifully fitted with couches and swivel chairs.

The fathers passed the time in a forward compartment playing cards, while in the rear their sons, rather green in complexion, kept the stewardess busy. Mary O'Connor herself, a wonderful woman who was United's chief stewardess and after whom Patterson's airplane was named, was in charge of the cabin.

After we landed, my father, who had begun flying for United in 1931, asked how I liked the trip. I said that I liked it a lot. He seemed surprised.

"They're not all that rough," he said.

I said I had figured that all flights were like that. He just laughed. What did I know? I was a ten-year-old kid who had just had his first airplane ride. But I wasn't too young to fall in love that night, and I dreamed of one day flying a DC-3.

Years passed, and I grew up, sort of. I learned to fly in an Army Flying Cub, became a professional photographer, bought an old Piper Super Cub, and eventually added multi-engine and instrument ratings to my commercial license. Still, I had never flown a DC-3, which was to my mind the most important airplane ever built, the airplane that brought air transportation to every corner of the world—the airplane that changed my life.

My dream remained a dream. I told myself

(Above and facing) The DC-3 and DC-3 engine. In most airline configurations, the DC-3 carried 21 passengers at 156 knots (179 m.p.h.). They were powered either by a pair of 1,200-h.p. Wright Cyclone R-1820 nine-cylinder radial engines or by 1,200-h.p. Pratt & Whitney Twin-Wasp 14-cylinder R-1830s turning Hamilton Standard props. The more popular Pratt & Whitney, shown here, ran more smoothly due to its larger number of cylinders. Both engines were very reliable, and like all radials, both always leak oil.

The "front office." For many pilots the DC-3 cockpit was home.

that one must be practical. To fly a DC-3 as pilot in command—or any airplane with a maximum gross weight exceeding 12,500 pounds or jet aircraft regardless of weight—a type-rating is required. The Federal Aviation Administration issues type-ratings for specific aircraft such as the Douglas DC-3 or Boeing 727 to pilots after they complete ground and flight instruction and then passing oral and written flight tests. (In the case of newer aircraft, sophisticated flight simulators are often used for the "flight" portion.) Since I did not intend to seek a job flying DC-3s, the time and expense required for a type-rating could not be justified. It would cost as much as a nice vacation and take just as long.

I was well into my thirties before realizing that while it was necessary to be practical, the only important things in my life had been done for love. Clearly, there was a need for some creative rationalization on this DC-3 matter. For example, how could one possibly compare the importance of a vacation against the deep satisfaction of making a dream come true? Ah, ha! That was it! Scratch one vacation.

Now the problem was logistics. Where do you go these days to learn to fly a 50-year-old airplane? I called a friend, Woody Woodhull, who just happened to be flying DC-3s for an airline in Florida at the time. (Old or not, DC-3s still

regularly carry passengers and freight all around the world.) Woody, who breathes aviation and flies like he has wings, agreed that getting the type-rating was not only more important than a vacation but more important than almost anything. He gave me some leads, and before long, they led to Trans-Florida Airlines in Daytona Beach. In addition to providing the regular ramp services, Trans-Florida flew charters using a Lockheed Constellation, Convair 240, and, of course, a DC-3. Most importantly, their training department offered the necessary ground and flight instruction for my coveted type-rating.

My instructor was to be Tom Kirton, a good-humored man whose gift for teaching, dedication, and love of flying are unmatched. We were about to spend an intensive week together, flying every morning and afternoon, weather permitting, with ground school in between and homework every night. If all went well, I would take an oral examination and type-rating check ride on the eighth day with an independent, FAA-designated examiner. Even though I was current on instrument flying and multi-engine procedures, my work was cut out for me. I had never flown anything larger than a light twin.

I flew to Daytona from New York the day before class was to begin, and in the late afternoon, taxied to the TFA ramp where Tom was waiting for me. I asked if I could sit in the DC-3 cockpit for a while to get used to where everything was.

The Trans-Florida airplane—N715F, Serial Number 4129—was powered by two nine-cylinder, 1,200-horsepower, Wright Cyclone 1820 radial engines; had a maximum gross weight of 25,200 pounds; and was originally delivered to Eastern Airlines in June 1941 as NC33643. Judging from what appeared to be plugged-up slit windows above the regular cabin windows, the ship must have originally been a sleeper with berths that made into beds for overnight trips.

Donald Douglas's DC-3, remember, was the flagship of its day when it first rolled out of his Santa Monica plant at Clover Field on December 17, 1935. In its normal cabin configuration, 21 passengers were whisked from city to city at an advertised 180 miles per hour—coast to coast in some 17 hours with only three stops.

Drafted during World War II, NC33643 was converted back to airline configuration and rejoined Eastern in 1947. With the exclusive registration of N1R, the ship became the Brooklyn Dodgers' team transport when Eastern sold it, and it later changed hands twice more before coming to Trans-Florida as N715F.

We climbed uphill past the empty passenger seats of the old tail dragger to the "front office," as pilots used to call the cockpit, and after pointing out a few things, Tom left me alone.

I eased into the left seat, wondering whether I had allowed the dream of flying a DC-3 to grow to the point where the reality could never match the fantasy. Yet as I sat with my left hand resting on the half-circle control wheel and my right on worn throttle-lever knobs, contemplating the old instrument panel with its hodge-podge of antiquated radios and instruments; as I looked through the narrow windshield that stood bolt upright so close to my face, wondering about the experiences of others who had occupied this same space; as I breathed the smell of cracked-leather pilot seats and aluminum seasoned with hydraulic fluid, oil, fuel, and sun, the airplane seemed to say, "I am everything you thought I'd be...." Thus began a dialogue between the Douglas transport and me that continued every day we flew and that I remember so clearly to this moment.

Now, before you start rolling your eyes, let me quickly say that I am not one of those romantics who contend that machines are alive. They have personalities, sure—kind, businesslike, sometimes bitchy—but that's all. Fuel and hydraulic fluid run through their arteries, not blood. But sometimes airplanes don't always fit strictly under the definition of "machine." Certainly DC-3s don't. For if ever there was an airplane that you could talk with, that stood by you with the heart and soul of a true friend, the DC-3 is it.

On the ramp before dawn the next morning, however, I was more apt to mutter to myself than to the airplane. Heaving the heavy Hamilton-Standard props through several rotations to clear the lower cylinders of accumulated oil is no easy task, even with Tom and me alternating blades.

"Could you show me that again, Tom?" I asked. "I'm not sure how to do it."

"Try the next six blades by yourself. You'll get the hang of it."

Red-faced and perspiring, we continued the walk-around inspection each morning, checking pretty much the same things as on a smaller airplane. Only the proportions were different. A ladder was needed to climb up on the wings, and a long, calibrated pole was used to check the quantity of fuel in the four tanks.

"Five hundred gallons left," I reported.

"That's plenty for today," Tom said. "We'll fill it tonight."

The oil dipsticks, accessible through little

doors in each engine nacelle, are marked in gallons rather than quarts: 25 maximum per engine of 60-weight molasses. Checking the landing gear is easy, because you can do it standing up with your head in the wheel wells just behind the engines. It was in there the first time that I learned you can't get near a big radial engine without its dripping oil on you. In fact, when they don't drip oil, something is wrong. Makes no difference how careful you are; engines are cunning. They save it up like a pigeon, then let go with a glob right on your nice shirt. I quickly invested in a special DC-3 wardrobe at the nearest K Mart.

So much has been written about starting radials that the descriptions have become clichés. But they are all true—the sounds, smells, shakes, snorts, and belching smoke; toggling the primer; hitting the booster-coil switch; switching on the magnetos after cranking six blades; craning your head out the window to check for fire. You feel you've accomplished something when you do it all just right, like waking up a teenager on a Saturday morning.

"What are you grinning about," Tom would ask after the smoke had cleared and the engines were rumbling along and the hydraulic accumulator was banging away behind us and the ship trembled, ready, in the first rays of a clear Florida sun. But he was smiling too.

There are a couple of other clichés that I found true for the DC-3: if you can taxi it, you can fly it, and it flies like a big Piper Cub. Part of the trick of taxiing is the brakes. They are toe brakes on the rudder pedals like most airplanes have, but these take some getting used to. It's like the first time you stomped on the power brakes of a '55 Chrysler and launched your Mom into the glove compartment. You soon acquire a heightened sensitivity in your toes and a deft touch on the throttles when maneuvering on the ground, especially in a crosswind or with the tail

wheel unlocked. The big vertical stabilizer that gives such good longitudinal stability in the air acts like a sail on the ground and tries to point you into the wind with considerable authority. I found that my previous tail-wheel experience, even though mostly in light aircraft, was of great benefit in coaxing the DC-3 to the run-up area. (Most modern aircraft have tricycle landing gears with nose wheels rather than tail wheels for easier handling during taxiing, takeoffs, and landings.) The principle is the same, only the inertia has changed.

Tom read the pre-takeoff checklist while I performed the tasks: controls free and clear; instruments set and showing the correct temperatures, pressures, and quantities; fuel selectors on the proper tanks; engine run-up, including checking the magnetos, carburetor heat, and propellers, all the while keeping my toes firmly against the brakes and the wheel hauled way back to prevent the tail from lifting during the engine check. As always, I took pleasure in the pre-flight ritual, because the only thing left to do after that was fly.

Lined up on the runway, tail wheel locked with the lever below the throttles, cowl flaps at trail, I brought up the power for my first takeoff—45.5 inches of manifold pressure and 2,500 revolutions per minute. It got noisy real fast, but everything else happened leisurely. With no passengers aboard, the tail soon came up by itself. Directional control was easy with such a big rudder. Tom, acting as copilot as well as instructor, signaled when we had accelerated to decision speed, while I kept my eyes on the runway, and at 84 knots, with the slightest back pressure on the wheel, we were airborne with acres of runway ahead unneeded. Sitting so close to the beak of the airplane with the windshield so near and the airspeed so low by present standards for an aircraft of this size, I felt like I was rising vertically in a level attitude, a sensation similar to that of taking a glass elevator at the Hyatt-Regency. After asking my copilot/teacher to retract the landing gear, I pulled the throttles back to METO (Maximum Except Takeoff) power—39.5 inches and 2,300 revolutions per minute—then passing through 1,000 feet to climb power of 31 inches and 2,100 revolutions per minute. We headed toward a practice area, climbing at 105 knots on up to 5,500 feet. There, I set the throttles to cruise power of 26 inches and 1,900 revolutions per minute, which produced a true airspeed of about 160 knots (184 miles per hour), burning 95 gallons of fuel per hour.

I felt at home in the airplane immediately, and during the next six days, we explored everything required for the type-rating and beyond: slow-flight (can you imaging flying an airplane that size at 60 knots indicated?), stalls, propeller feathering and unfeathering, aborted takeoffs after the tail was up, go-arounds, various instrument approaches, VOR and ADF radio navigation intercepts, and holding patterns (intensive work with only one crank-tuned receiver of each type). These exercises were always performed under the hood, a visor worn by student pilots to limit their view to just the instrument panel, thereby simulating an instrument flight. And always, of course, my diligent instructor would simulate an engine failure by suddenly cutting the power on one engine at the most inopportune moments. Tom was relentless, but with good-natured enthusiasm and a fiendish sense of humor. I don't think either of us had ever worked harder or had had more fun under such an intensive schedule.

After one simulated engine failure, Tom covered the artificial horizon and directional gyros with pieces of paper. I was under the hood, and since these are the two primary instruments for blind flying, I had to rely on the more primitive turn-and-bank indicator to keep things right side up.

"Your gyros just ran down," Tom said with pleasure.

"My gyros ran down?" I puzzled that one while scanning the remaining instruments with great interest. Partial-panel flying, as it is called, keeps you on your toes. Considered an emergency today, the turn-and-bank, airspeed indicator, and altimeter were all the early instrument pilots had.

The main gyros are driven by vacuum. Tom was obviously simulating a vacuum failure causing me to use the electrically driven turn-and-bank. A total vacuum failure would be

View from the pilot's window. Some DC-3s still carry passengers 52 years after first entering airline service. Counting both commercial and military versions, 10,926 DC-3s were built.

unusual, however, since there are two pumps, one on each engine, either of which will run the gyros. I looked at the vacuum-pump selector switch. Of course, dummy, I said to myself. It was set for the left pump, and sneaky Tom, knowing that, failed the left engine. Part of the engine-failure procedure is to check that the selector is set for the working pump. Tom had failed the engine just as I was entering a holding pattern and knew I might be preoccupied enough with the added work load of the simulated emergency to neglect the pump selector. I turned the selector to the right pump, and Tom uncovered the gyros.

"I'll get you for that, Kirton," I said. Nothing had gotten out of hand, but a lesson was driven home by a little extra sweat.

During all of our training, the DC-3 handled predictably, honestly, and with character and dignity. Progress may have brought with it benefits in speed and comfort, but there has never been a flying machine with more integrity than the DC-3.

On the morning of the eighth day, I felt prepared, but there is always the unknown in taking a check ride. Mr. Tacker, my FAA-designated examiner, would also act as my copilot since part of the examination involved judging a new captain's use of his crew. Tom would ride in the jump seat behind us.

Tacker was a tall, lanky fellow, who appeared to be in his fifties and who didn't say too much, kind of hard to read. On the way to the airplane, though, a Twin Beech passed by on takeoff, tail wheel dangling from the short-coupled fuselage, and Pratt & Whitneys hammering away. Another survivor from the 1930s, the Beech Model 18 has been everywhere and done everything, but it is also known to be a handful at times. Tacker squinted up at it affectionately.

"I learned to fly in one of those," he said. At first I took him literally and was surprised,

because the Twin Beech would eat up a new student.

"You mean you began flight training in a Beech 18?" I couldn't believe it.

"No, but I learned *fly* in one," he said. I knew then we'd get along.

Tom had prepared me well for the check ride, and Tacker was certainly thorough but fair in both the oral and flight examinations. Everything went smoothly until the last maneuver, a VOR, circling approach under the hood to a relatively short runway. Tacker had simulated an engine failure just before we reached the VOR, but I managed to get through the engine-out procedure (including switching the vacuum-pump selector) and still pick up the correct radial to the airport. At approach minimums I yanked off the hood to land visually, simulating breaking out under the overcast in actual instrument weather. We were in close and to the left of the airport, as we were supposed to be. This particular procedure called for a right circling turn to line up with the runway, but as a result the runway was difficult to see from the left seat of such a big airplane until banking to begin the circle. My mistake was in delaying the final descent too long for fear of getting too low too soon with an engine out.

Turning toward the runway, it became clear that I was in a box. We were too high to touch down on the runway threshold, and the runway was too short to permit landing any farther down than that. A right circling approach to a short runway with an engine out is one of the more demanding challenges in a large airplane, a fact that was not lost on Tacker. He had chosen this spot for the last exercise. The DC-3 and I knew there was only one good way to salvage the landing, but I didn't know what Tacker's reaction would be.

"We're too high," I shouted over the noise of the good engine, "and the runway is too short to land long. I'm playing like this is the real thing with a heavy load of passengers in the rear. A go-around attempt on one engine would be crazy."

While talking I cranked in a hefty amount of left aileron with the control wheel in order to drop the left wing and pushed right rudder to keep the old girl from turning. The resulting slip bled off the excess altitude quickly without increasing airspeed. It was indeed just like flying a big Cub, but it was not standard procedure in transport aircraft.

Slipping was a frequently used maneuver in the early days, especially before aircraft had as effective wing flaps as they do now. Many light planes, and even some transports like the Ford Trimotor, had no flaps at all.

My examiner kept his hands in his lap and didn't say a word. Leveling out just before the runway, I planted the main wheels on the threshold for a normal landing. Whether Tacker would flunk me for being too high or pass me for recovering by the seat of my pants was anybody's guess.

"Let's go back to Daytona," said Tacker. On the way we talked about the weather. Finally, after shutting down on the Trans-Florida ramp, I could no longer stand the suspense.

"Well, did I pass?" I asked.

"Sure you passed," my examiner said, and he began filling out a temporary certificate for type-rating.

"The government used to print 'Douglas DC-3' when they added the rating to your license," he said. "Now they just write 'DC-3' to save space. I've always liked it better with 'Douglas,' so that's what I've written on your temporary certificate, even though they'll take it out when they mail your permanent ticket in a few weeks."

"Thanks, Mr. Tacker. I'll save it." He must have understood why I'd come to Florida. He felt the same as I did about DC-3s.

My log book still shows only 13.5 hours of DC-3 time. I haven't had the pleasure of flying one since, and I can't claim great knowledge or experience in piloting the airplane. I didn't fly it over the "Hump"—the Himalayan Mountains—for the Army Air Corps in World War II nor land it at Wilkes Barre, Pennsylvania, in a 40-knot crosswind with blowing snow for American Airlines. But in learning to fly the DC-3, I touched an important part of aviation history. I flew the greatest plane ever made. For that kid who always dreamed of flying one, it meant everything.

(Right) A DC-3 still in service as a freighter. (Overleaf, pages 86-87) The AgCat. Designed by Grumman, now built by Schweizer, the AgCat was conceived solely for aerial application.

(Above) After World War II, Stearman trainers could be bought surplus for very little money. Many were converted to crop dusters by putting a chemical hopper in place of the front cockpit. Some still serve in that role, but as their antique value continues to rise, more are being restored back to "two holers." (Facing) A Stearman fertilizing a rice field flashes by a flagman, who gives the pilot an aiming point for each swath. Overhead wires are a constant danger for aerial applicators.

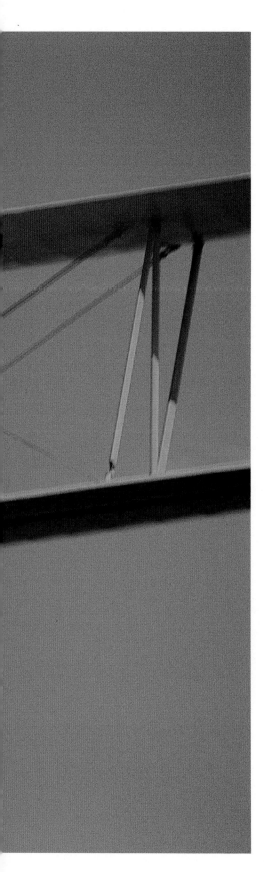

(Above) Ayers Turbo-Thrush. Powered by a Pratt & Whitney PT-6 turboprop engine and extremely capable, the Turbo-Thrush is a far cry from a Stearman. This particular Ayers is one of a handful supplied to the government as a Narcotics Eradication Delivery System (NEDS). It has 1,376 s.h.p. and, appropriately enough, self-sealing fuel tanks and an armor plate around the pilot's seat. (Facing) A Stearman spreading fertilizer pellets. (Overleaf, pages 92-93) AgCat at work in Texas.

*(Above and facing) Cessna Turbo 206 bringing
supplies and mail to an isolated ranch strip on
Idaho's Salmon River.*

(Above) A bush pilot. (Facing) DeHavilland DHC-2 Beaver on final approach to a Canadian lake. As in all flying, weather is critical to the bush operator. With fewer weather-reporting stations in back country, a bush pilot may not know whether he will return from a trip the same day or a week later. (Overleaf, pages 98-99) Cessna 180. On wheels or floats, Cessna 180s and 185s (similar except for engines) are rugged workhorses.

(Above and facing) DeHavilland Beaver bringing supplies to a Hydro Quebec camp in northern Quebec. Powered by a Pratt & Whitney 450-h.p. radial engine, the deHavilland of Canada DHC-2 Beaver is unquestionably the finest bush plane ever made. Although out of production for years, they are in constant demand.

(Below) An ex-Navy Grumman S-2 spreading retardant on a California forest fire. (Facing) Consolidated PBY Catalina. Converted to a fire bomber, this aging former-Navy flying boat is a grand old lady who deserves a less strenuous life.

Piper PA-18-150 Super Cub on skis in Vermont.

A Mooney after being caught out on the ramp during an ice storm.

(Above) A weary bush pilot waiting for his deHavilland DHC-3 Otter to be loaded. (Facing) With the evidence of many years and thousands of hours on its worn rudder pedals, this Curtiss C-46 still soldiers on, hauling freight to Central America.

(Above) Crop duster's helmet and goggles after a day that began and ended in twilight. (Facing) DeHavilland of Canada DHC-3 Otter on floats. Built longer and with a more powerful 600-h.p. Pratt & Whitney R-1340 engine, the Otter is the Beaver's big brother. (Overleaf, pages 110-111) Davis-Monthan storage area.

TIME SUSPENDED:

A DESERT REST HOME FOR AIRPLANES

(Left) Insignia painted on B-52 0003, the X-15 mother ship. (Facing) Airplanes awaiting new life at Davis Monthan.

From a distance the shapes looked like shark fins in a smooth sea. There appeared to be hundreds. Some shone silver in the morning light, others an uneasy black. But they didn't move. It was as if someone had shouted "Freeze," and all activity, even the passage of time, halted abruptly. Strange things happen in the desert.

Geologists say that this ground five miles southeast of Tucson, Arizona, was an ocean bed at one time. Now it lies in dry desolation, inhabited by coyotes, prairie dogs, lizards, and creatures of an altogether different kind. Walking up a gentle rise for a better view, a visitor sees that the fins do not belong to prehistoric sea life but to a species of "Bomberus Obsoletus" called the Boeing B-52.

With thousands of other aircraft, they were being stored at the Military Aircraft Storage and Disposition Center (MASDC to the government) at Davis-Monthan Air Force Base. Few places on earth are as suitable for an airplane rest home, because the two main causes of mechanical deterioration—rust and corrosion—are almost absent in the dry air and alkaline soil of the Tucson desert.

The sight of those machines suspended in time and placed in orderly rows seems unreal. I had seen them from the air on previous trips but was always in too much of a hurry to stop. This time I did.

Most of the some 4,000 aircraft residing on the 3,000 acres flew in under their own power when they were no longer needed by the military. About half will someday fly again. For the rest, life will slowly drain away in a trickle of spare parts donated to still active ships, and when everything of value has been stripped, the desecrated carcasses will be sold as scrap and melted down for recycling. It's sad to think that the precious skin of the gutsy F-16 blistering by overhead may one day wrap last night's fish. Some of us might wish that all airplanes could fly forever, but as taxpayers we can at least rest assured that MASDC is getting the most from what we paid for.

Upon arrival every aircraft undergoes a preservation procedure. Fuel systems are drained and coated with light oil; hydraulic systems and tires receive normal servicing at regular intervals; and guns, classified equipment, and pilferable items are removed. Then intakes and exhausts, cracks and gaps, canopies, radomes, and ports are papered, taped, and sprayed with a vinyl plastic called Spraylat that not only completes the seal but eliminates damaging interior heat from the sun. The lower half of the fuselages are left unsealed so that air may circulate to prevent condensation. Each craft is then towed to its assigned spot and tied down on the hard caliche soil to await the call. Computers keep track

Convair T-29 cockpit.

of what is where and which parts, if any, have been removed.

Walking through the quiet rows of aircraft is a haunting experience. I wondered where each had been, who had flown it, and what pilot and plane had seen together. Moving slowly, stopping here and there, I examined the young and old; the faceless and famous; the flashy, short lived superachievers and the less dramatic but consistent, long time performers. With character showing through its homely features, the reliable Grumman S-2 and derivatives were present in abundance, sturdy and reliable as ever. B-52s, many still wearing Vietnam war paint, seemed to be everywhere.

A little farther off, three special aircraft—called the Boeing Holy Trinity by MASDC personnel—rested in dignity side by side. One was N70700, the famous 707 and KC-135 prototype, still adorned in the 1950s-style paint scheme that was seen in all the publicity photographs when Boeing announced the first U.S. jet airliner in 1955. N70700 had led a long and productive life, even serving as the 727 test bed with a fifth jet rudely stuffed in its tail. Now back in its original configuration, this historic ship has been donated to the Smithsonian Air and Space Museum in Washington, D.C.

A few feet away stood a modified B-52 sporting a gust probe attached to a long, nose-mounted boom and canard control surfaces on the forward fuselage. This is the control-configured vehicle used to research the B-1 flight-control system. Looking like it had just landed a few minutes ago, the NB-52E is ready for its next assignment.

The third member of the Trinity—one of the most famous B-52s of all—was nestled between the other two. It was the third Stratofortress built, a B-52A, and because of its nose number—0003—it was called Balls 03 in its final role. Also known as the High and Mighty One, it was already five years old when it became one of two X-15 mother ships, the aircraft that carried the rocket planes to altitude for launch.

Seen in all the news reels, 0003 served

"Streaker's" Grumman S-2.

faithfully in one of the most successful aeronautical research programs ever undertaken. There was a notch cut out on the right-wing inboard trailing edge to accommodate the X-15's vertical fin, and further forward under the wing, the pylon that firmly held the craft suspended was still in place, as well as numerous camera ports to film each drop from every angle. With its unusual cargo in place, the B-52 could not lower takeoff flaps, requiring a dramatically longer and faster run than normal and a delicate touch on the controls by its pilots. I walked closer to where I remembered from photographs that the X-15 cockpit had hung. Its windshield would have been just about at my eye level. My view of the B-52 must have been the same one that test pilot Scott Crossfield had seen on the morning of March 10, 1959, when he went aloft in the X-15 for the first time. Combat bombers have bomb symbols painted on their sides to mark each mission; Balls 03 had a row of X-15 silhouettes stenciled on it to proudly record each launch.

The variety of aircraft stored at MASDC would quicken the pulse of the most casual observer. Across the way from the three Boeing sisters are the YC-14 and YC-15 prototypes, both looking as if they had just rolled out of the factory door. These aerodynamically sophisticated troop carriers made by McDonnell Douglas and Boeing, respectively, were created as part of a design contest to build a replacement for the able Lockheed C-130. Because of budget cutbacks, a contract was never awarded. Now they sit side by side like Olympic athletes waiting for the judges' decision. Surrounding rows of aircraft include T-38s resting on pedestals like desk models; once exotic RB-57s, C-130s, A4s, and U-8s; Cobras, Voodoos, and Jolly Green Giants; not to mention Presidential helicopters from at least three administrations.

Off by itself, an old Sikorsky UH-34 helo with Texas Air National Guard markings caught my eye. The rotors had been removed and bundled alongside the landing gear, and it appeared that the machine would never fly again. Inside were the dusty remains of an executive interior with a couch and, next to the big picture window, a comfortable, individual chair. President Lyndon Johnson had sat there on many occasions when flying between his ranch in Johnson City, Texas, and Air Force One parked in Austin.

For me, the most poignant part of MASDC was an area called the Back Forty, because the end is in sight for machines parked here. Parts have been stripped, and some are already broken up for the smelter. It was deadly quiet when I walked through in late afternoon. I heard a groan of scraping metal and looked up to see a B-52 stabilator pulse slowly upward and down in a gust of wind—a moan and twitch like an old, sleeping dog dreaming of glories long past. With the balancing weight of their heavy engines removed, some of the prop ships had rocked back on their main wheels, noses pointed skyward, poised for a takeoff that would never come. Birds twittered about, landing on a wing tip or tail fin, then fluttering off again as if coaxing these once-proud ships to get back in the air where they belonged.

It was eerie. I had the feeling each ship had a life story just like you and me. I wished there was some way I could listen to them tell their tales; that I could sit beneath the KC-97's wing and hear about the time Lieutenant Kramer had to land her during a white-out in Alaska, or learn what the RB-57 saw on those secret reconnaissance flights when Captain Smith flew her so high she teetered on the very edge of her limits.

The stories were floating in the desert air, I know. I could almost hear them, like snippets of a conversation that is just out of earshot.

B-52 being stripped for the smelter.

A cocooned Grumman S-2 engine. This 1,525-h.p. nine-cylinder Wright R-1820 will fly again.

(Above) McDonnell Douglas YC-15 prototype. (Overleaf, pages 120-121) Boeing KC-97 poised for a takeoff that will never come.

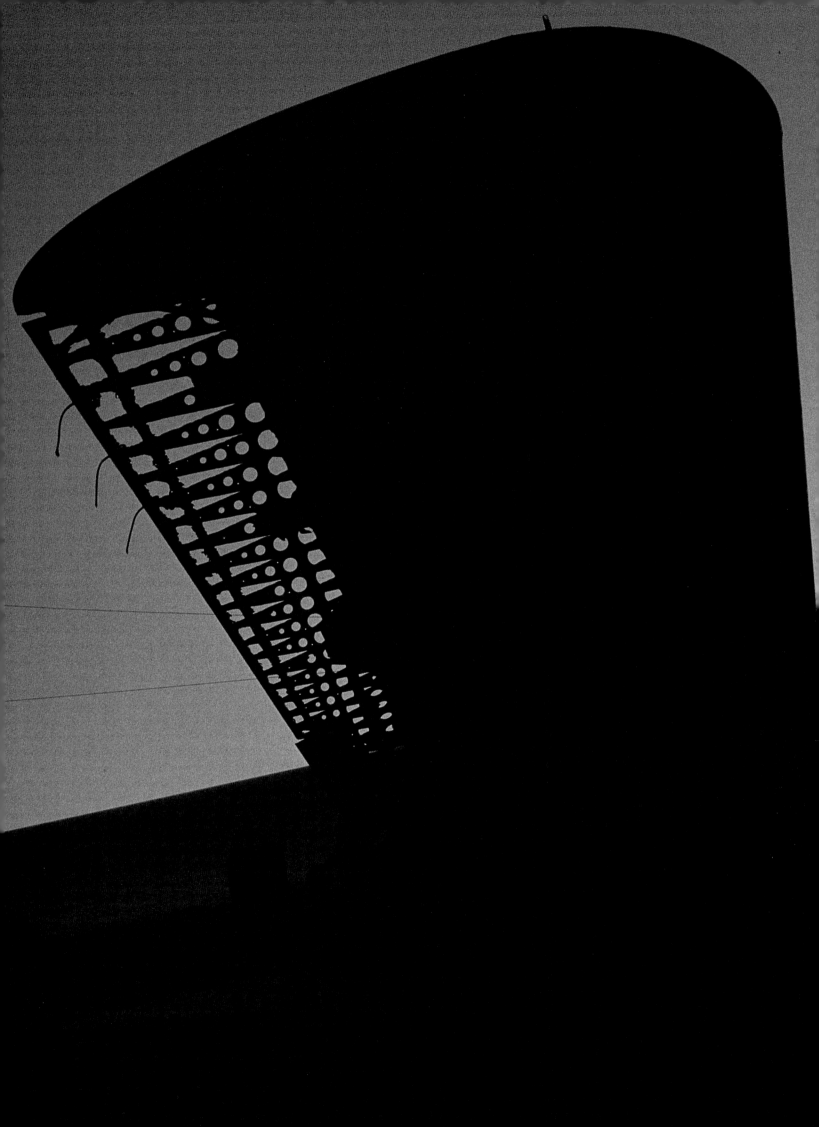

(Above) Jeff Michael in "Obsession." (Overleaf, pages 124-125) Ford 5-AT-74 Trimotor. N414H first flew in 1929. It is now powered by three 450-h.p. Pratt & Whitney R-985 radial engines and cruises at about 90 knots (104 m.p.h.).

JEFF MICHAEL

I went crazy the first time I saw an airplane. My dad, who learned to fly on the G.I. Bill right after World War II, had an N3N back when I was about six years old. He and a friend of his took me for my first airplane ride in a Luscombe about that time. I kind of got addicted.

My dad had a service station where I worked washing cars on Saturdays. Then I'd take the $5.00 that I had earned to the airport on Sunday and take a 30-minute flying lesson. I sold my bicycle, sold my model airplanes, and everything I could sell to get another five bucks for a flying lesson. It's been a good investment.

Not long ago I bought the very airplane I learned to fly in. It's a 65-horse, old rag-wing Luscombe. A friend of mine had it, and it hadn't been flown for 14 years. The Luscombe's a fun little airplane, and of course, this one played a big part in my life. I had taught myself spins, snap rolls, and loops in it as a student pilot when I was seventeen, still in high school.

My early flying was literally grassroots. I built up my time flying mostly out of grass strips. Got my private license when I was eighteen; then went up to Winston, North Carolina, when I was nineteen and got my commercial license and instructor's rating. After that I taught for a while at various airports until I got a job with Piedmont Airline's fixed-base operation in Winston as an instructor and charter pilot. At that time it was a good stepping stone to the airline, and I moved over to Piedmont's airline division in 1965.

I started out flying as copilot in Martin 404s,

worked my way up to captain, and recently moved to the 767, which is a big thrill to fly because it's such a good performer. I may be tired of motel rooms, but I still enjoy the heck out of airline flying. Going to work is always a pleasure.

When I was a kid, I used to hear the guys talking about the P-51 fighters and all that they did during World War II. People who flew them were heroes. The P-51 was always one of *the* airplanes to fly. Still is. It became one of my life's goals to have one. You look at that thing, and it makes you want to jump in it, like it's saying, "Come on." It looks like it wants to fly. It also looks kind of wicked. It's strange in a way, being both beautiful and wicked. It lures you right into it. That's exactly what it does.

I couldn't afford one for a long time, so I bought an old Ryan PT-22 that I had two engine failures in, then three Stearmans in a row, then a North American T-6 that I still have today.

When I went to pick up the T-6 in New Orleans, I had only ridden in the back seat of one before. The fellow I bought it from asked, "You ever flown one of these things before?"

"No, but I've flown Stearmans a lot, and I've been reading Len Morgan's T-6 book."

"Well, you won't have any trouble," he told me. So I just hopped in the airplane and took off. I keep it on a little 1,800-foot grass strip on the farm where I live.

Around 1970 or 1972, I started flying airshows in the T-6. I'm not a professional airshow pilot by any means, but I got my unlimited aerobatic waiver from the FAA and just enjoy doing it. I fly about seven shows a year.

Over the years I had just about given up the idea of ever owning a P-51, because the price kept going up all the time. Finally, I figured out a way to do it. It was worth waiting for.

Even today the P-51's performance is outstanding. When that thing's running right, it sounds like a sewing machine from the cockpit.

It kind of hums inside. Visibility is excellent, and the control response seems automatic. Every time I fly it, I feel how lucky I am, lucky that I finally got to do something I've always wanted to do. I wish everybody else could have the same experience.

I fly airshows in the Mustang too. There are often guys who'll stop by to talk who actually flew P-51s in the war. It's fun talking to people who really were there, and like I said, World War II pilots were my heroes. They ask questions, and I ask questions, and I get a lot of information from them. I really enjoy talking to them. Many of them haven't seen a P-51 since they got out of the service 40 years before.

One time one of those guys was looking at the airplane, and I could tell he wanted to see inside. I put him in the cockpit, and you could see by his expression that he was getting emotional about it. When he got back out of the airplane, I asked him if the one he flew during the war had had a name. "Yeah, Patty Ann," he said. The tears started coming down his face, you know, and it made me almost cry too. He had known from reading the newspaper that a Mustang was going to be there that day, so he had brought out his combat records and everything to show me. Things like that make it all worthwhile.

I named the P-51 "Obsession." That's exactly what it is. I built a lot of my life around getting one, altered my lifestyle, and did everything I could to work out a way to do it. My goal now is to keep it. These things get more and more expensive to have, and I suppose there might be some point down the road when I will have to get rid of it. But I'll always be thankful for the privilege I've had in owning one.

—Jeff Michael, Airline Captain,
Lexington, North Carolina

(Above) Ford Trimotor fold-down wing baggage bin. Those fat wings produce tremendous lift with plenty of room inside for fuel and bags. (Right and facing) Ford Trimotor passenger cabin and flying over Nevada.

A 1931 Pitcairn PCA-2 Autogiro. This is the only flyable example of the PCA-2. Owned and flown here by Steve Pitcairn, son of the founder of Pitcairn Aircraft Company, the ship was carefully rebuilt by autogiro expert George Townson. Powered by a 300-h.p. Wright R-970, the machine is still a spectacular performer.

Beechcraft D18S control wheel.

Spartan 7-W Executive. The beautiful Executive began production in 1937, but only 34 were built before the company shifted its attention to the coming war effort. A competitor to the Beechcraft D17S Staggerwing, the Executive was comparable in performance and powered by the same 450-h.p. Pratt & Whitney engine. It carried four to five people at 175 knots (201 m.p.h.).

(Above) Stinson SM6000B Trimotor. The Stinson trimotor was introduced in 1929 and was smaller than the Ford. It carried 10 passengers at 85 knots (98 m.p.h.) powered by three 215-h.p. Lycoming R680 radial engines. NC 11170, shown here, was built in 1931 and flew for a time with Century Airlines. Eventually the aircraft was abandoned in Alaska and rotted until it was rebuilt by Chuck Andreas, Bill Brennand, and Byron Frederickson. It is flown here by Brennand and Hasson Calloway. (Facing) "You can't go wrong with a Wright". This one is mounted on the Pitcairn autogiro.

Curtiss C-46 Commando. Originally conceived as a plush airliner before World War II, the C-46 gained fame during the war by hauling cargo over the Hump, the aerial supply route across the Himalayan mountains between India and China. When it was built, the C-46 was the largest twin-engine cargo plane in the world. Powered by two 18-cylinder Pratt & Whitney R-2800 engines, the beast cruised at 170 knots (196 m.p.h.). "Tinker Bell" belongs to the Confederate Air Force and is kept operational by Chet Brakefield, Dave Cummins, and Sublet Scott.

(Clockwise from top) "Tinker Bell" flown by Len Morgan and Dave Cummings; Chet Brakefield, master physician of old airplanes; and a Martin B-26 Marauder cranking up. (Overleaf, pages 136-137) Martin B-26 Marauder. The only flyable Martin B-26 in the world is owned by the Confederate Air Force and flown here by J.K. West. The Martin medium bomber was considered a handful when it joined the Air Corps in 1942. Training accidents were so numerous at MacDill Field in Florida that the phrase, "One a day in Tampa Bay," was coined. In combat, however, the B-26 had a lower loss rate than any American bomber in Europe, and many crews grew to respect the beautiful Martin as she brought them back home again and again.

(Top) Curtiss P-40. (Bottom) Harper Buck, former B-24 bomber pilot, in front of the only flying B-24. It is owned by the Confederate Air Force, which performs an invaluable service to aviation history by collecting, maintaining, and flying World War II aircraft. (Facing) North American P-51D. There are three airplanes that any vicarious fighter pilot dreams of flying: the Spitfire, the P-38 Lightning, and the P-51 Mustang. Certainly one of the most beautiful planes ever made, the Mustang is powered by a 1,590-h.p. 12-cylinder Rolls-Royce Merlin V1650-7 liquid-cooled engine. P-51s have a top speed of 385 knots (443 m.p.h.). (Overleaf, pages 140-141) Martin B-26 before a dawn takeoff.

(Above) Nancy Bink in her Grumman American Traveler. (Overleaf, pages 144-145) Eipper-Formance MX ultralight just after sunrise near Manteo, North Carolina.

NANCY BINK

When I was changing careers, I took a class, and one of the things we were asked to do was make a list of 10 things that described us. One of mine was "pilot."

I had never really given flying much thought as a kid. When I was about ten or eleven years old on a family vacation in the White Mountains, we took a sightseeing ride in a small plane. I don't remember much about it except that we were flying over farmland. I didn't think about flying again until I was in college. A boyfriend had asked me what was the one thing I'd always wanted to do, and what I heard come out of my mouth was, "I've always wanted to fly." I thought, "Now wait a minute…really?" So I must have been thinking about it all along. That

was when I actually realized that flying was something I really, really wanted to do.

My friend took me out to a soaring club in Pittsburgh, and we went soaring. It was terrific. That was the first time in my adult life that I had gone up in an airplane other than an airliner.

After that I think I may have gone to an Aero Club meeting in college, but I didn't really pursue flying for a while, because I didn't have the money. Then in Boston three or four years later, I was bored with myself. I had a little savings in the bank, and I said, "I want to do something memorable with this. I think I'll learn how to fly." I opened the Yellow Pages, picked out a flight school, and that was that.

After the first demo flight where the flight-school instructor let me take the controls, I was totally hooked. It took about a year to get my license, because I was working and had to fit lessons in on the weekends. There was no doubt in my mind that I would go through with it.

I always thought flying was incredibly exciting, but I don't think I realized how much work it would be, studying and understanding things about airplanes that I didn't expect I'd have to know. I'd thought learning how to fly a plane would be similar to learning how to drive a car; someone puts you in it, shows you where everything is, and off you go. Instead I was learning about how a piston engine works. It was great.

After I got my license, I rented planes from the flight school. A couple of years before, my father had also earned his license; he was about fifty. It was something he had always wanted to do, and my mother had given him lessons for Christmas one year. He then bought a Grumman Traveler, which he liked very much. There was some talk about me being allowed to fly his airplane, so I went to another airport and learned how to fly Grummans. I joined a club there, where I flew Cheetahs and Tigers for a long time. After a while, my father decided he didn't fly enough to justify owning a plane, so he sold the Grumman to me. I fly it on weekends for fun.

When I was still living in Boston, my airplane was ideal for traveling. Nantucket, Martha's Vineyard, Block Island—all those places were close by and flying to them took 45 minutes to an hour. It was so easy that I would take all my friends on day trips there.

Now that I'm in New York, I can't do that anymore, but I don't mind just flying around for the fun of it. That's what I wanted to learn to fly for anyway. I don't really care to add more ratings or buy a faster airplane; I just like having the method to get up in the air. I like the machinery of it too.

When someone asked me what I was most proud of doing, I said, "Getting my pilot's license." It's the best thing I've ever done, the smartest thing I've ever done, and the most challenging thing I've ever done. Other than my home, family, and friends, I can't think of anything that means more to me than flying. It is out of the ordinary. It gives me a sense of accomplishment.

The main reason I fly is that there is something about the perspective you get when you fly that alters your view of the world. If I move somewhere new, for example, the first thing I do is fly over the area to see what it's like. And I say, "Ah...so that's what it's like. That's where I've moved."

You don't know what you're looking at as much when you see it from the ground. When you're in the air, you get a whole different perspective. I fly over my house all the time, look at the driveway, look at the garden. Maybe it doesn't make sense to say that flying changes your perspective on life, but it does. It shifts how you see the world. Being suspended up in the air seems like such a great place to be, such a normal place to be, even though you realize that a hundred years ago nobody was doing it. But it seems so natural that you think being up in the air is really where you should be spending most of your life; the ground, a place to go down to when you have to.

—Nancy Bink, Art Director, New York

(Above) The pilot's seat of an Eipper-Formance MX over the Manteo, North Carolina, airport. (Facing) A 22-h.p. single-cylinder two-cycle Xenoah 250-cc engine mounted on a Vector 610 ultralight aircraft. Who said a snowmobile engine can't fly?

RAPTURE OF THE HEIGHTS:
AN ULTRALIGHT ADVENTURE

Beware, dear son of my heart, lest in thy new-found power thou seekest even the gates of Olympus.... These wings may bring thy freedom but may also come thy death.

—Daedalus to Icarus, after teaching his son to use his new wings of wax and feathers.

I had a nagging suspicion all morning that the Manteo, North Carolina, forecast was wrong. It said one thing, the facts said another, but no one in officialdom was bothering to reconcile the difference.

Leveling the Bonanza at 5,000 feet after a noon IFR (Instrument Flight Rules) departure from Teterboro, New Jersey, I found that the promised 350-degree, 20-knot tail wind was closer to a 120-degree head wind. This confirmed my doubts about the forecast. A low-pressure center parked off the Carolina Outer Banks apparently had the impudence to ignore the Weather Service computer's suggestion that it move northeastward. No matter. If the current weather held for two more hours, it would still be above minimums for Manteo's VOR approach on my arrival. If not, Norfolk was a solid-gold alternate with much better weather and an ILS approach.

The weather en route was benign. Not a single blip appeared on the Stormscope, and the clouds that soon engulfed my airplane obligingly remained two degrees above freezing. No bumps and no ice. Conditions were perfect to sit back in my cozy cocoon and enjoy the intimate, abstract beauty of instrument flying in a small airplane. The experience is at times monotonous and fascinating, and at least part of the fascination lies in placing oneself in a potentially hostile place and returning safely by the disciplined application of knowledge. Perhaps practical and efficient aerial transportation was developed solely for pilots to amuse themselves.

My purpose in going to Manteo was to fly an Eipper-Formance Quicksilver MX ultralight aircraft, quite the opposite of the machine that was taking me there. An ultralight by definition can weigh no more than 250 pounds nor cruise faster than 55 miles per hour. The early ones were hang gliders powered by chain-saw engines. To its supporters, the ultralight was the latest answer to the ageless quest for an Everyperson's Airplane. It could be built from a kit, stored in a garage, and in the beginning, at least, flown without a license or even the benefit of flight instruction. To its critics, the machine was at best a joke and at worst dangerous. No one denied that they were quite a thrill. I had to fly one.

Burrowing through the clouds at 200 miles per hour in my comfortable, sophisticated Beechcraft, I wondered how my years of piloting "real" airplanes would apply to going aloft in a flying lawn chair. This most basic of flying machines would soon give me the answer in a very humbling way.

Elizabeth City, North Carolina, 31 miles northwest of Manteo, was the closest weather-reporting station to the uncontrolled airport of my destination. As I flew over, descending for Manteo, Elizabeth City was reporting broken clouds at 700 feet, 2,500 broken, good visibility underneath, and strong, northeasterly surface winds gusting to 35 knots. Air Traffic Control cleared me for a VOR-16 approach with a circle to land on Runway 4. Closer to Manteo, which is surrounded by water, the ceiling became overcast with occasional breaks. Minimum ceiling for this approach was 740 feet, which was almost precisely where I broke out of the clouds into a leaden, gusty world with white caps below and the airport in sight. Weather forecasting still leaves something to be desired, computers notwithstanding. Instead of the anticipated one-hour-and-55-minute trip, with perhaps 10 minutes of actual instrument time, it turned out to be two hours and 20 minutes, with an hour and a half on the gauges. A routine trip in unthreatening weather, yet immensely satisfying.

Two days passed before the weather was suitable for ultralight flying, providing me with a good opportunity to get to know my host, John Harris, president of Kitty Hawk Kites. John is an old hang-glider hand. Since 1974 he and his staff have taught more than 75,000 adventurous folks to fly hang gliders on the sand dune across the street from his shop in Nags Head, North Carolina. About 70 years earlier, the Wright Brothers used to hang glide on their own sand dune in Kitty Hawk, just a hop, skip, and a jump north of Nags Head, so it's old stuff down there.

At the time of my visit, Harris had expanded his business to include the sale, service, and training for Eipper-Formance (get it?) ultralights, one of the largest manufacturers of the machines. Like all responsible ultralight dealers, Kitty Hawk Kites included a training program with each sale.

The thought had crossed my mind that perhaps ultralights were nothing more than impractical toys, a cheap thrill which, by virtue of an engine, was longer in duration than that

provided by a parachute. To find out Rob Bickerstaffe, then Harris's chief ultralight instructor, introduced me to the Quicksilver MX. The machine, having been removed from its trailer and assembled in 40 minutes, stood on the Manteo ramp all brightly colored with wings set at a jaunty dihedral. It looked as eager to fly as I was.

"It sounds funny, but the MX is a slow, high-performance airplane," said Bickerstaffe. "The controls are very responsive, and the 30-horsepower Cuyuna engine makes the takeoff and climb fantastic."

While I strapped in and squeezed on a crash helmet, Rob explained where everything was. The two-cycle, two-cylinder engine with manual recoil starter, as in a lawn mower, was above and behind me. It turned a geared pusher-prop sticking out behind. Over my head, straddling a structural member, rested a semi-opaque, three-gallon, plastic bottle. That was the fuel tank. Mounted on the left-forward vertical support tube was an on-off switch and a twist-grip, motorcycle-style throttle control. A side-mounted control stick sat to the right of the single seat, which was bolted to exposed tubing.

There was no enclosure for the pilot and no instrumentation of any kind except for a crude airspeed indicator. This Mickey Mouse device consisted of a clear plastic cylinder within which a yellow disc floated at various levels depending on the velocity of air entering the cylinder from a forward-facing intake at its bottom. The outside of the cylinder was etched vertically with numbers. If the yellow disc in flight hovers around Number 30, say, that is your airspeed. Simple? Yes. Cheap? Very. Reliable? Hmm.

Originally designed for snowmobiles and adapted for ultralights, the U.S.-made Cuyuna engine has a reputation for reliability, durability, and easy starting. Compared to the paperweights that powered some of the earlier ultralights, that wasn't saying much, but in my experience the engine was powerful and ran smoothly.

While the Quicksilver MX had a full three-axis control system, it differed slightly from that of a conventional airplane. Fore-and-aft movement of the stick controlled the elevator as usual, but lateral stick moved the rudder, and the foot pedals operated spoilers on either wing that could be used separately for roll or simultaneously by depressing both pedals for glide-path control. This welcome feature added an extra measure of agility, and apparently the designers felt the simplest way of achieving it was to activate the spoilers with the pedals. For airplane pilots used to having the rudder controlled by the pedals, this took some getting used to. Later models adopted the conventional airplane standard.

Rob began my transition training with taxiing. Since the MX is a single-seater, my instructor stood halfway down an inactive taxiway to watch my progress. Excellent rudder response made taxiing easy. I was already having fun. Performing a 180 at the end of the pavement was another matter, however. It takes room and planning since the nose wheel is not steerable. Slowing down enough to turn reduces rudder authority because of less airflow around it. The solution is to give a blast of power to throw prop wash over the rudder. It works, but the throttle must be reduced almost immediately to prevent the aircraft from gaining too much speed. But then the rudder loses effectiveness again, so you give another blast, but.... Well, you eventually get used to it. If you have planned poorly as I did at first, you just roll to a stop (brakes are optional), put your feet on the ground beneath your seat, lift with your legs, and tippy-toe around to the desired heading. It is awkward, un-birdmanlike, and often accompanied by guffaws from onlookers, but it is better than

The infamous ultralight airspeed indicator.

running into something. Later models have steerable nosewheels.

Rob next asked me to taxi straight ahead at a faster speed sufficient to just hold the nosewheel off the ground and roll on the mains. We were getting closer to the real thing. The air-speed indicator showed about 22 miles per hour. Each time I ran over a bump or was hit by a puff of wind, the airplane skipped clear off the ground momentarily. It was on the verge of changing from go-cart to flying machine.

We took a break to refuel the small tank, adding the mixture of automobile gas and oil demanded by two-cycle engines. Next on the agenda were short hops, two or three feet off the ground, where I learned to adapt to the non-standard rudder and spoiler control.

"I'm going to walk down the runway," Bickerstaffe said an hour and a half after we had begun. "Take off and hold it level at five feet. If everything looks good when you pass me, I'll wave you on, and you can take it up and have some fun."

This was it, what I had been waiting for since the first moment I saw the Quicksilver. With more excitement than my first solo, I lined up on the runway and slowly opened the throttle. To feel this little, flexing creature—this alliance of aluminum tubes, stainless-steel cables, and dacron—gather itself up and lift into the air is soul-stirring, for it instantly unites its smiling, wind-swept pilot with everything that has ever

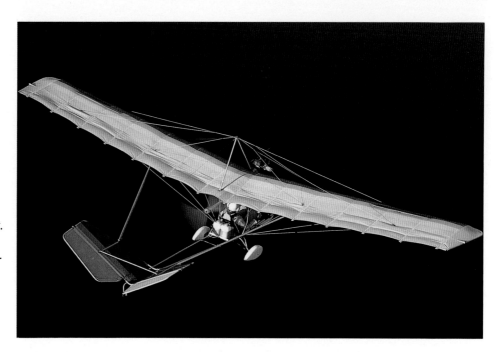

(Right) Vector 610 ultralight. (Overleaf, pages 152-153) Eipper-Formance MX ultralights flying by the Wright Brothers Memorial at Kitty Hawk, North Carolina.

flown and everything that ever will. It is thrilling all right, but it isn't a cheap thrill. It reaches all the way down.

I throttled back to maintain five feet over the runway. Rob waved and I opened the throttle fully. The machine sprang upward like it had been kicked in the pants. I had hardly climbed above tree-top level when I saw the Wright Brother Memorial at Kitty Hawk five miles to the northeast. There, 79 years before, the Wright brothers had risen above the sand in a contraption not much cruder than the one in which I now flew.

At approximately 1,000 feet (with no instrumentation, everything is approximate), I tried gentle turns with the rudder only, as Rob had suggested, until I became familiar with the machine. The airplane has so much dihedral that any skidding is hardly noticed. My instructor was right; the MX is a slow, high-performance airplane. An intermediate power setting gave an indicated 40- to 45-miles-per-hour cruise speed. The little kite is delightful in the air, responsive, and light on the controls. I was soon wheeling about, climbing and descending, absolutely ecstatic. This must have been what Icarus felt, I thought.

Descending to shoot a landing, I found the spoilers quite useful to lose altitude more quickly. Thirty to 35 miles per hour seemed a comfortable speed on the approach, and as Rob had instructed, I held a little power and flew it on the runway in a slight nose-high altitude. Full-stall landings are out; the tail skid will probably hit first, and the airplane tends to bounce. Power-off stalling speed is about 23 miles per hour, and a normal touchdown occurs at around 25. The landing roll is ridiculously short, under 100 feet, and the takeoff run even less.

Climbing back to altitude, I noticed my air-speed indicator was holding an amazingly steady 30 miles per hour. That didn't seem right. I was climbing at a conservative angle and would have expected to see something more like 40. I twisted the throttle grip to make sure it was fully open. It was. The engine sounded healthy. I lowered the nose to gain speed. The yellow disc remained at 30. I raised the nose to lose speed. The disc was unmoved, and unmoveable. It was stuck. Ah well, do birds need air-speed indicators? I climbed on up to play some more, not realizing that the wax holding my feathers was about to melt. I had never been so carried away with flight. The Quicksilver was like a motorcycle with wings.

I decided to shoot more landings and circled outside the traffic pattern at about 500 feet waiting for another of Kitty Hawk's ultralights to land and back-taxi to where Harris and Bickerstaffe were standing. It looked like they were bringing out gas cans to refuel. Dear God! I looked up at the fuel tank. A thimbleful of gas remained. I checked my watch in disbelief. With no fuel gauge, you must time yourself against the known fuel consumption. What I had guessed to be 15 minutes aloft was actually 45. I was having so much fun that I lost track of time. Stupid.

By then I had reentered the pattern on an extended base leg over the trees that surrounded much of the airport. I knew that if the engine quit, I would never make the runway. It quit.

I put the nose down and turned toward the airport hoping to reach a grassy area within its boundary. The MX glides more steeply than one might imagine, more steeply than a Bonanza, for example, because of the high drag from the many bracing wires and exposed tubing. The air-speed indicator continued to display its frozen lie, so I relied on all the feel I had acquired from hundreds of power-off landings in Cubs to select an angle of attack that neither mushed nor dove the airplane. This would give the maximum gliding distance, and I would need all I could get. How many times had I said that only fools run out of gas? Now I had proved it.

"Beware, dear son of my heart...." Too late, Dad. I had allowed myself to fall victim to that most insidious of all diseases: Rapture of the Heights. My intense pleasure had distracted me from realizing that ultralights are "real" airplanes too and demand the same presence of mind from their pilots as any other airplane. As long as I am being honest, I might as well add that despite the urgency of the situation, I have never felt more alive or more aware of my senses than I did during those moments. Knowing that it would be hard to hurt myself in a 23-mile-per-hour impact as long as I kept control, I was still having fun—deadly serious fun, but fun nevertheless.

The trees slipped by below me, so I crossed off the possibility of mushing into them. Ahead lay a field of tree stumps, then a drainage ditch immediately preceeding a taxiway running perpendicular to my path. Beyond that lay the grass. In slow motion each obstacle passed by until my main wheels touched down on the taxiway and I coasted across it onto the grass. I got out and began pushing the machine toward my companions who were running over to me.

"Nice landing," Bickerstaffe said charitably.

"You're looking at an idiot," I replied.

The sun had already set by then, preventing my flying again that evening. It had been a thought-provoking experience, my first engine failure on my first ultralight flight. I have always been a cautious pilot on every detail from walk-arounds to weather, yet I had just pulled the most thoughtless of blunders. How could that be? It was a serious error that only the guardian angel of fools permitted to pass without consequence. Similar lapses of awareness in more critical circumstances have struck down better pilots than I. I placed myself on probation.

A pure, intense dawn shone the next day on an appreciative but wiser Icarus who floated in the chilly morning air 1,000 feet, approximately, above the flickering glints of light on the water. This flight in the Quicksilver was like a final dip in the sea on the last day of vacation.

Rejoining the world of procedure and regulation began with a lengthy telephone call to the Flight Service Station to file an IFR flight plan back to Teterboro. I took off, called Washington Center, waved good-bye to the Wright Memorial, and gave full attention to the tasks at hand: turning on the pitot heat in the snow showers, copying amended clearances, double-checking fuel consumption, navigating accurately, and all the other little things that pilots must stay aware of. In two hours I was listening to the endlessly busy Teterboro controllers for landing clearance.

Serious airplanes, fun airplanes, I love you all, but I will never forget again that even fun airplanes must be taken seriously.

(Above) Henry Hampton with his Beechcraft Sundowner. (Overleaf, pages 156-157) From the rear seat of an LK sailplane being towed aloft. The LK was formerly a World War II training glider.

HENRY HAMPTON

Istarted building plastic model airplanes when I was ten or eleven and read whatever I could find about aviation. I was just enamored of it. There was some aviation lore in my family too. My uncle, Reginald Woolridge, was one of the first black pilots with the Army Air Corps during World War II. He was originally an artillery officer, then was trained to be an observation pilot. I remember him stopping by in his uniform to see us. He later received a medical discharge because of flak injuries but was able to get back in the service. At one point after Korea, he became the oldest rated helicopter pilot in the Army. He is an interesting guy, and I realized that if he could fly, one day I could too.

Flying to me was always a terribly enticing

dream; you know, the idea that you could do it and what would it feel like. I remember my first solo as almost anti-climactic, because I had envisioned this feeling for so long. I still dream about flying.

My actually learning to fly was delayed by polio. By the time I got out of the wheelchair and got rid of the crutches, I was a sophomore in college. There was an airport just west of St. Louis by the river called Lobmaster Field. I took lessons there and soloed in a Tri-Champion. At that point they didn't have hand controls yet. I wear a full brace on my left leg, but I just sort of worked it out for myself. I did my cross-countries in a Tri-Pacer.

Things got busy at school right after that, so

I didn't get my license then, but I remember my parents being very supportive of my flying, because they knew it was something I cared passionately about. It gave me the extra dimension of being able to run, so to speak, even though physically I couldn't.

For the next 15 years, I could only fly intermittently because of work and money. Then one weekend in New Hampshire, I went to the airport to see a friend of mine who was taking up soaring. While watching him, I started talking to a woman named Shirley Mahn. She had been a WASP during the war, had umpteen-thousand hours, and was one of those people who loves flying viscerally. They named a beacon after her right near the Twin Mountain Airport. She said, "Come on up." We hopped in a Warrior, and everything came rushing back.

I was living in Boston then, and a friend that I used to play wheelchair basketball with had his own airplane, a Cherokee. He said, "Take the airplane." I found an instructor and started building up hours. After going through a special review to get a waiver of demonstrated ability because of my leg, I got my license a year later. That was around 1976. My company was growing by then, so I bought a used Beech Sundowner and began to fly a lot for business. I still have that plane.

Flying is one of those human activities that in some ways duplicates the most precious parts of what makes us human. Expectation is one of those, one of the great distinguishing characteristics of the human animal. We can anticipate. The wonderful thing about flying is the moment before takeoff, when you're sitting there, and it's all in front of you, and the flight is about to be made. Then comes the exhilara-tion when the wheels cut loose. To me, it's one of the greatest pleasures. That's when my mind shifts gears, and everything else sort of drops away. I'm thinking only about what's going on with the airplane and what's above. It's a great cleansing pill. When I haven't flown for a while, I feel like I need to go do it.

Flying is a wonderful combination of physicality and spirit. I can't imagine not flying. It would be one of the worst sadnesses of my life if I couldn't. I'm going to hang onto an airplane as long as I am able. Every once in a while, I will pick up the Sundowner's key and subconsciously rub it a little, wondering what it would be like to jump in the plane on the spur of the moment and fly to the Vineyard, or Nantucket, or just climb up to 4,000 feet, especially at night, circle around, and get right with the world.

There are some things you do when you're hurt or frightened that bring you back together again. Flight is one of those for me. I use it like an old friend. When I found out that my mother had died, I went out and got in the airplane and just flew around.

Flight has visual impact too, just like a good film, and it has pacing: a beginning, middle, and an end. It has drama. It has color.

I've never seen two sunsets quite alike. Flight offers one pleasure after another: the way the land looks at 1,500 feet, the way it looks at 10,000. And you love to share it, to introduce someone else to it.

—Henry Hampton, Television Producer,
Boston, Massachusetts

(Below) Classic LK sailplane flown by Bob Roe landing at Estrella Sailport south of Phoenix. (Facing) A Sisu 1A sailplane, of which only 10 were built, soaring over the California desert near El Mirage. Here it is piloted by owner William Ivans.

DeHavilland D.H. 82A Tiger Moth. The two-place, open-cockpit Tiger Moth was Great Britain's most widely used trainer from the late 1930s through World War II. Many Royal Air Force heroes earned their wings in Tiger Moths. Powered by a 130-h.p. Gipsy-Major engine, many of these delightful airplanes have been lovingly restored and are still flying throughout the world.

160

(Left) The Royal Jordanian Falcons aerobatic team in their Pitts Specials. (Below) Airshow performer Jim Holland flying Tigre, his Pitts S-2A. Designed by Curtis Pitts especially for aerobatic competition, Pitts aircraft are superb performers.
(Overleaf, pages 162-163) A rare and beautiful Meyers OTW. Designed as a trainer for the Civilian Pilot Training program prior to World War II, Al Meyers' OTW (Out To Win) was powered by a 145-h.p. seven-cylinder Warner Scarab radial engine and cruised at 90 knots (104 m.p.h.). The OTW was unusual in having an all metal fuselage mated with fabric-covered wings and horizontal stabilizer. About half of the 102 OTWs built still exist today.

(Above) Prop hub of a Lycoming-powered Piper J3 Cub. (Right) Even a Staggerwing landing gear makes a fascinating work of sculpture. (Facing) Beechcraft Staggerwing B17L, Serial Number 3. All of the Model-17 Staggerwing variations, B through G, are collector's items today. NC 270Y, pictured here, was the first production aircraft sold by Walter Beech's new Beechcraft company. It first flew on February 2, 1934, powered by a 225-h.p. Jacobs L4 engine, which provided a cruising speed of 130 knots (150 m.p.h.), quite remarkable for the time, especially considering its low landing speed of 39 knots (45 m.p.h.). NC 270Y flew actively for 15 years but eventually was left to decay outside a garage near San Francisco. It flew again on August 27, 1982, having been restored from a basket case by the two men seen here in the cockpit, Dick Hansen and Dick Perry, and their crew. The Beechcraft Corporation now owns the airplane.

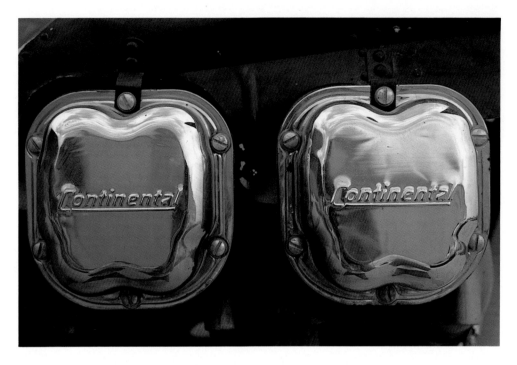

(Top) Chromed rocker-box covers of a 65-h.p. Continental engine. (Bottom) Elegant simplicity is reflected in the design of this 1940 Piper J5A Cub Coupe. Three generations of the Everts family in Miami have owned and flown this particular J5 since it was new.

(Above and overleaf, pages 168-169) Beechcraft D18S. Called the Twin Beech, the Model 18 was the premier corporate transport from its introduction in 1937 until the turboprop Beech King Air came out in 1964. The last Model 18, a Super H18S, left the Wichita factory in 1969 after 32 years of continuous production. Powered by two 450-h.p. Pratt & Whitneys, the D18S, flown here by Dub Yarbrough and owner John Parish, carried five to seven passengers at a typical cruising speed of 174 knots (200 m.p.h.). Because of its short-coupled tail-wheel landing-gear configuration, the Twin Beech could be a bear to land or take off in strong cross-winds, but she was revered by those who mastered her.

(Above) Bob Loomis and his Cessna 172. (Overleaf, pages 172-173) Piper PA-18-150 Super Cub. A Super Cub is the aerial equivalent of a Jeep. It was designed to live in the back country; operate out of short, rough strips; and require little maintenance. Powered by a 150-h.p. Lycoming engine, it lands at a slow 37 knots (43 m.p.h.) and cruises at a modest 91 knots (105 m.p.h.). It carries two people and a hefty load slowly and with considerable noise, but boy is it fun.

ROBERT LOOMIS

When I was maybe five or six, a Ford Trimotor landed in a pasture at Conneaut, Ohio, giving rides. My dad bought me the copilot's seat, so I got to sit up front. That was my first airplane ride, and I never forgot it. Nobody in my family flew except my uncle down in Plain City, Ohio. Back in the 1920s when he was young, he built a plane in his dining room. He couldn't get it out, and of course, it wouldn't have flown anyway—but all during my childhood, I remember its gigantic wooden propeller lying on the rafters in the barn.

My uncle became an avid weekend pilot. He had a 2,100-foot grass strip right by his auto agency, and he always had an Aircoupe or some other light plane and took me for rides when we visited. His partner had an old Bonanza that I would go out and just sit in for hours.

There wasn't anyone else in my home town interested in aviation when I was growing up, so all my flying was vicarious except for those family trips to Plain City.

Do you remember those Assen Jordanoff books? YOUR WINGS and the others? I read those books over and over again. I drew and designed thousands of airplanes as a kid and built model airplanes from the time I could open the glue.

In the 1950s—after I'd moved to New York and was working as a book editor—Piper had what they called a Press Plane at Safair Flying Service at Teterboro Airport in New Jersey. It was a Tri-Pacer, and rented for $10 an hour, including gasoline—or $15 an hour with an instructor—I learned to fly in that airplane. Teterboro was busy even then, so students had to deal with fairly sophisticated radio work and a good deal of traffic, which was a blessing in disguise. I took a bus from Manhattan to Teterboro at six in the morning, flew for an hour, and then took the bus back in time to go to work.

After I got my license, I bought my first airplane, a 1956 Cessna 172, and took brief trips to places like Flying W Ranch in New Jersey for lunch with my wife and daughter. The 172 was a good airplane, but by then I really wanted to travel, and so I traded it in for a C-model Bonanza. With 60 gallons of fuel, you could go almost anywhere in comfort, and we did.

Still, the Bonanza is an expensive airplane to keep up, so I bought a 1964 172. I flew it on a 6,000-mile trip around the United States alone, VFR. No question about it, that was one of the most memorable things I've ever done. I knew where I wanted to go in general, but I didn't have to be anywhere on a certain date. I went south, then across Texas into the Southwest, up to Wyoming, and finally straight back through the Midwest—but on no set course. There was something new each day. I could fly as far as I wanted, dawn to dusk, or just hop 200 miles and tie down again. The weather, of course, was the major unpredictable element. Once I got stuck in Arkansas for three days, but somehow I remember even that with some nostalgia. A trip like that dramatically demonstrates what a privilege it is to be able to fly around this country. It's an experience that can't adequately be described to someone else.

After the second 172, I bought another old Bonanza and kept it for 10 years. Then I got a little Alon Aircoupe that was perfect for local flying until my son was born, and I needed more seats again. I looked around for a year for the perfect airplane—once again, the 172 was the answer. I found a really mint 1956 model for only $10,000. It even had an auxiliary tank and a remanufactured engine. In many ways, it's perfect for what I need now, flying around the Northeast from Long Island, over to Martha's Vineyard, or up to Connecticut.

Why do I fly? The simple answer is because I've always wanted to. Why that desire was there is something I can't answer, but I do know that flying itself has always lived up to my excitement about wanting to do it.

Physically and mechanically, of course, an airplane is fascinating. It's really a grownup's toy. Its beauty comes from a design that is almost entirely functional, and I get a great deal of pleasure out of the precision necessary to make a good flight.

Part of the appeal is also spatial, because when I was a kid, long before I ever flew, I used to think what it would be like to take off right over the trees like a bird. There's a freedom of movement involved, coupled with a slight anxiety, that makes flying an experience like nothing else.

And there's always the possibility of the unexpected that gives you a sense of heightened awareness. You're in an unnatural environment, high above everything, and your mind is always occupied about where you are and what is happening, even when you're flying across a spectacularly barren place like west Texas, with nothing to look at but a tiny house every 10 miles or so.

If I flew every day, I'd probably get used to sitting up there, but since I don't, it remains a very special thing. There's something satisfying about flying that I don't get from anything else. Just a simple thing like making a good landing makes me feel good for a couple of hours. Sometimes in the summer I'll go out to the airport and fly twice a day, even just for five minutes. And if it's raining I'll go out sometimes and just sit in the damned thing.

—*Robert Loomis, Book Editor,*
New York City

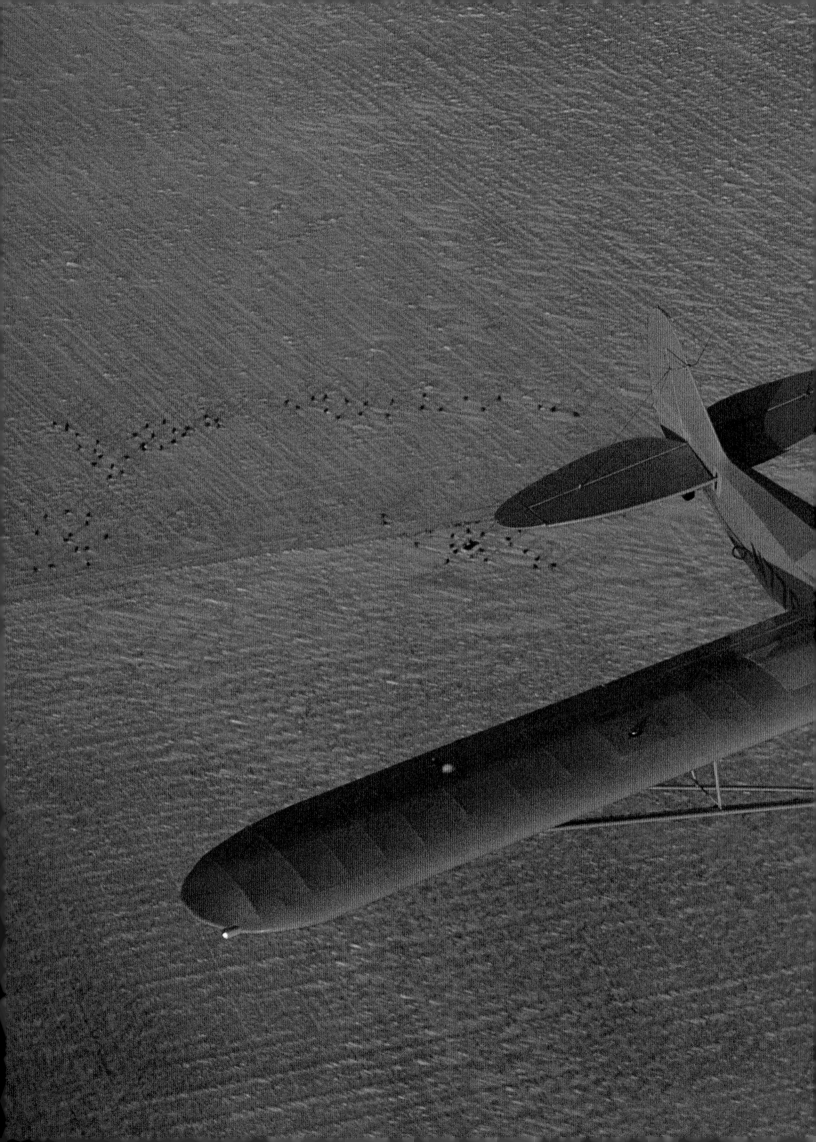

CROSS-COUNTRY CUB: THE FREEDOM TO GO

(Right and facing) A Super Cub's nose and view.

The dream of having your own plane is a dream of freedom: the freedom to take wing, to see the familiar from a different perspective, to go wherever you wish whenever you wish. Translating the dream into hardware can take many forms, from home-builts to business jets. Each is a compromise, because machines are more cumbersome than dreams. One will do a particular job well at the expense of something else. If an aircraft flies very fast, it can't fly very slow. If a plane can't fly very slow, it can't land on short strips; the list of variables is long. Designers have worked miracles in juggling tradeoffs, but no airplane will take you wherever, whenever without limitation. Dreams have the advantage there.

Nevertheless, most of us still require a machine to get off the ground, so we select an airplane that best suits our needs and pocketbooks. If you want to roll your own, a home-built is the answer. Some come in kit form, and others are built from scratch using detailed plans.

Of course, the fastest, most comfortable, and certainly the most chic way to get from Point A to Point B is via that ultimate of all status symbols—the business jet. In addition to owning the jet, though, it helps if you also own the corporation that picks up the tab for operating it. Even so, these marvelous jewels of aeronautical ingenuity—and they are truly beautiful—have their own particular drawbacks too, just like anything else.

For example, you don't barrel off low across the country at 500 miles per hour in your jet, landing anywhere you feel like it. Like airliners, they are flown at high altitudes where they are most efficient and on necessarily more restrictive instrument flight plans as required in airspace above 18,000 feet. Airports they use must have runways of adequate length, and most jets require a crew of two in the cockpit. There is a price for being able to go that fast. In general, the more sophisticated the airplane, the more removed you are in many ways from that dream we were talking about.

The determining question, really, is why do you want to fly? We customarily speak of airplanes in terms of going places, especially on business, as if their existence must be justified by a bottom-line purpose. As far as I am concerned, the sky is the only important place airplanes go. What better reason for flying could there be than for the sake of flight itself? After all, fast, efficient air transportation is only a useful by-product of the Wright Brothers' wonderful invention. A by-product that just happened to change the world, to be sure, but it all started with a dream.

My dream of flight is exactly the opposite of that provided by a sealed, silent, pressurized, climate-controlled jet. For me, flight in its freest form, the kind of flight that puts you in closest touch with the sky, is experienced more fully in a simple stick-and-rudder airplane. Many of those you may see at the airport have been around for decades, with decades of life yet left in them. Others, like the Christen Husky, are brand new.

The one that suits me most is the old Piper Super Cub I've had for 20 years. It is slow, noisy, and old-fashioned: a fabric-covered, two-seat tandem, tail-wheel airplane that cruises at a leisurely 100 miles an hour; has windows on the left and a clamshell window/door on the right, all of which can be left open in flight; and is an absolute joy to fly.

Because they still do some outback jobs better than more modern designs, Super Cubs remain in production 50 years after their lower-powered, look-alike ancestor, the J3 Cub, first rolled off the line in Lock Haven, Pennsylvania. Reliable as sunrise, the Super Cub is the Jeep of airplanes that will get in and out of the most rudimentary air strips as long as you're in no hurry. With a slow, 43-miles-per-hour stall speed and windows that open, they are ideal for aerial photography.

But usefulness aside, I just happen to be partial to old tail draggers: ships like Aeroncas, Stinsons, early Cessnas, and Pipers. They are trusty machines that you can jump into and go when you feel like it. Autopilots? Weather radars? These aged pelicans have never heard of that stuff, but as a result, they give the pleasure of flight in greater measure than the latest bizjet.

About once a year, usually in the spring, I get a powerful urge to fly the Cub out west. (It generally takes a year for me to forget how sore my rear end got on the last week-long trek to Arizona.) For flyers or photographers, the southwestern United States is surreal. The weather is almost always good, and the landscape holds you in constant meditation. With a slow cruising speed, the usual head winds going

westbound, and the inevitable weather delays encountered on long, VFR (Visual Flight Rules) trips, one could drive to Arizona as quickly. But that is a minor price to pay for the beauty to be seen from my little bird.

To travel more efficiently, the only way to go is in a faster, IFR (Instrument Flight Rules)-equipped airplane so that you can plow through the clouds on a schedule. The tradeoff is that you fly higher, don't see as much, and fly on a rigid flight plan talking to air-traffic controllers all along the way.

Weather conditions, aircraft radio and navigation equipment, and pilot qualification determine whether or not you go IFR. In weather below VFR minimums (three miles visibility and a cloud ceiling of 1,000 feet in controlled airspace), you must either sit on the ground until the weather improves or, assuming the plane is properly equipped and the pilot is instrument-rated and current, file an IFR flight plan.

Instrument flying is a different environment and necessarily more regimented. It is interesting, challenging, and sometimes beautiful, but to me, it is rarely as much fun as the other kind of IFR—"I Follow Roads"—navigating with the radios off and a thumb on the map. Getting there, as they say, is half the fun.

Every student pilot learns map-reading skills for navigation by pilotage, which means confirming your position by identifying the features on the ground that are marked on the map: towns, rivers, roads, race tracks, quarries, schools, mountain peaks, or any other noticeable, and some not so noticeable, visual cues.

Radio navigation is so much easier, a simple matter of tuning the receiver from one VOR (VHF Omnirange) station to the next and following the needle like a dummy, such that the keen edge of pilotage skill is soon dulled from lack of exercise. LORAN-C radio navigation, made

Evolved from the Piper J3 Cub of 1938, Super Cubs are still in production today.

practical for small planes by the microchip, is even more seductive than omni. You tell the receiver your destination, and it tells you the heading, distance, and time it will take you to get there as it constantly updates your ground speed en route. Satellite navigation will be another improvement when it arrives soon.

With such miraculous electronics available, one easily forgets that you can get practically anywhere on earth with a map, compass, and watch. Besides, radio navigation charts are dull to look at. They don't show terrain, only symbols for navigation stations, airports, airways, intersections, and other data. In contrast, aeronautical sectional charts, used for pilotage, are in themselves colorful objects of beauty. Showing topography and cultural features in detail, they are wonderfully informative of the land below, in addition to displaying airports, airspace restrictions, and all other necessary aeronautical information for VFR flight. It is good to stay proficient in using them too, because they always work. Radios don't.

Non-flyers look quizzical when you say you're going to fly voluntarily from New York to Arizona in a Piper Cub. "How long will it take," they ask, and, "Where will you stay along the way?"

The answer to both is, "I don't know."

"Sounds exciting," they say. Those with adventurous souls mean it; others mean, "Sounds boring as hell."

In planning a long, VFR flight, you start by keeping close track of the weather several days in advance. The Weather Channel on cable television is excellent for this. Each season has its own weather moods: winter is aggressive; summer, lazy; fall, restless; spring, tempestuous. Each has its own particular rhythms and crosscurrents. As you approach your proposed date of departure, which may or may not be the day you actually leave, you observe the weather systems moving west to east across the country, see how fast they're moving and what kind of weather they're bringing. It's like standing on the seashore in order to study the timing and strength of the breaking waves before you dive in. The best time to leave is right after a system has gone through, so that you have a stretch of good flying weather. Because the weather is hardly ever clear all the way to your destination on long trips, you must leave as soon as you can and get as far as possible.

I left May 28th on my most recent trip, departing East Hampton, which is near the eastern end of Long Island, on a sunny, late morning after light ground fog had burned off. Leveling off at 1,000 feet, I headed toward the northern Long Island shore so that I would be in position to circumnavigate the New York Terminal Control Area (TCA) to the north when I got closer to the Big Apple.

TCAs are upside down wedding cakes of positive-control airspace that surround all major airports in the country. Nothing flies within them without the permission and assigned altitudes and headings by air-traffic controllers. My Cub has an altitude-encoding transponder and all the required goodies to get a clearance through the TCA, but there is less hassle just to go around it. So I angled northwestward as I approached its core, staying south of Westchester County Airport's traffic area further to the north and below the overhanging layers of the TCA above me.

Monitoring the radio conversations between controllers and aircraft in the TCA from outside, as well as requesting clearance through it, gave me a good idea of traffic flow. During slack periods the controllers will give radar traffic advisories to aircraft outside the TCA if requested, but during busy times they can't. Even though you may not be in controlled airspace, it is a good idea to listen in anyway whenever you're nearby and to always have your transponder on so that you can be seen easily on the controllers' radar. Like the little girl in the movie *The Exorcist*, your head must be on a constant swivel, looking for other airplanes. I go out of my way to avoid high-density traffic areas whenever possible.

Harrisburg, Pennsylvania, is a good place to stop for gas. Traffic is never heavy at Capital City Airport, and the terminal restaurant is just a short walk from the fixed-base operator (FBO), where I refueled and called Phillipsburg Flight Service Station, the nearest one, for a weather update. Flight Service Stations are run by the Federal Aviation Administration and located at selected airports in all regions of the country. They accept flight plans (mandatory for IFR flights, optional for VFR), provide weather briefings, and give other information of interest to pilots. Communication is by telephone, aircraft radio, or in person. Whenever possible, in-person briefings are best, because you can study the various weather maps and charts firsthand and then talk it over with the briefer.

A slow-moving, low-pressure area, I was told, remained far to the west, but it was

Super Cubs may not be the fastest way to travel, but they afford superb views, such as this one of a foggy river in early morning.

extensive and already spreading high clouds and moist air into western Pennsylvania. The weather was still good VFR, but visibilities were expected to lower toward evening as the temperature dropped closer to the dew point. Back in the Cub, I chugged off, following the Pennsylvania Turnpike, my high-tech nav-aid, with several possible destinations in mind where I could spend the night, depending on how long the visibility held up.

Westbound from Harrisburg, the first of several Allegheny Mountain ridges soon crops up across the route. In good weather they look benign, with tree-covered ridges and lovely green valleys spotted by small towns in between. To a westerner the ridges aren't high—3,500 feet will top them all—but as the airmail pilots found out in the early 1920s, they're treacherous little devils when the weather is down. For one thing, the ridges curve from the southwest to the northeast, which is disorienting, and the valleys all have a similar look. It was easy to get lost flying along, down low, with the mist in the trees, no forward visibility, eyes straining over the side of the open cockpit, hoping for a familiar landmark. Once lost, it was even easier to miss seeing the ridges camouflaged in gray until they loomed quickly into darker gray and suddenly into a startling, rushing, terrifying presence of tree limbs and rocks. Airmail pilots hit the ridges with regularity before the days of instrument flying. Passing over the first ridge, I thought about those brave men, too many of whom had died to prove the concept of airmail. And I thought, too, of the occasional impatient pilot, who even today tries to sneak through the Alleghenies visually in IFR weather and meets the same fate but without the redemption of being a pioneer.

The turnpike goes through tunnels in four of the ridges, and just on the western side of the third, the Tuscarora Tunnel, at the floor of the ridge, is the small grass strip that attracts me every time I fly over. It is marked on the sectional chart as Burnt Cabins. No house sits nearby, no hangar, no windsock, no fuel pumps, and I have never seen an airplane on it, yet it is always nicely mowed. There are many such strips in the Midwest, but they are situated on farms with houses close by. Does the owner of Burnt Cabins commute from it everyday, explaining the absence of the plane when I have flown over? Is it on a larger piece of land owned by an absentee landlord who comes by air to check on it now and then? Is there a shed that I didn't notice, where an old Aeronca Champ is stashed and flown each evening by a pilot watching the valley turn from bright green, to golden green, to purple green, and finally to a throaty, dark, blue green before returning to land in the twilight?

One day I'll land at Burnt Cabins for a stretch and look around, maybe walk a couple of miles to the speck of a town that bears the same name and try to find the owner of the airstrip. I want to tell him or her how much that stretch of grass has fired my curiosity over the years.

Weather tends to linger in rumpled terrain, and I hoped to get past the Alleghenies before the system to the west forced me to stop for the day. Western Pennsylvania was looking fuzzier as I flew on. The lowering sun had disappeared behind thickening clouds, and I knew from talking on the radio with Pittsburgh Flight Service to the north that the velvety haze should hold at the present three to four miles until sunset, then turn to ground fog in the valleys by morning.

Now past the roughest terrain, I studied the sectional to find an airport among my possible destinations that was on reasonably high ground; I didn't want to be trapped in valley fog the next morning. Washington, Pennsylvania, just east of the Ohio border, looked good. My Aircraft Owners and Pilots Association (AOPA) Airport Directory said there were motels nearby. I hooked left at New Stanton where Route 70 forks off from the turnpike.

The head winds had slackened to the point where I was whizzing past the cars below at probably a 25-mile-per-hour speed advantage. Such speed is intoxicating, but I had to be alert for a four-lane highway heading south. Washington and its airport should be just a spit down that road. Turning left on what I thought was the correct road, I soon discovered that Washington wasn't there, so it was back to Route 70 for a closer look at the map. Ah ha. I wanted the second four-lane to the left, not the first. I must be getting tired. Four miles further, hidden in the haze, was the correct road. Another left, and the airport appeared right where the map said it would be.

In the five hours, 26 minutes of flying time I spent getting from East Hampton to Washington, an airliner could have flown coast to coast. But that would have been routine. This was an adventure.

"Where you from?" asked the lineman refueling the plane.

"East Hampton, Long Island."

"That's a long way in a Cub. Where you headed?"

"Arizona."

"I've always wanted to do that. Just get in one of our planes and go somewhere."

"Why don't you?"

"Maybe I will. Next vacation."

Our country is fortunate to be spotted with hundreds of small airports like Washington: one paved runway, fuel and maintenance service, taxis and car rentals, an instrument approach for bad weather, flying lessons, plane rentals, and private planes—everything you need. No control tower exists, because the amount of traffic doesn't warrant it.

A community of 18,000 is far too small to be of interest to the airlines, but an airport opens such a town to the large, general aviation transportation system, comprising aircraft operated by private individuals and corporations. Airline-type airports are important, but so are the small ones like Washington.

My high-ground trick worked, and the next morning I took off with good visibility while the nearby valleys were still socked in. A weather briefer at Flight Service had told me I wouldn't get far VFR, and he was right. The low-pressure area was practically stalled in eastern Indiana. I had hoped to get as far as Dayton, Ohio, but had to stop 20 miles short at Springfield, Ohio, only two hours and five minutes from Washington. Beyond Springfield, the weather turned black and wet.

Springfield Municipal, three miles south of town, has long runways and enough general-aviation and commuter traffic to need a control tower. Radio contact is necessary at controlled fields before entering the traffic area, so I called 15 miles out to get the numbers.

"Super Cub 7789P, winds 240 at 12," a voice reported over my radio. "Lightning visible to the west. Report base leg for Runway 24. Hawker-Siddley jet on final. No other reported traffic."

"Rog, 89P," I responded. The lightning report I had just been given let me know not to dawdle, but with light wind and no mention of gusts, the thunderstorm was not yet close enough to the airport to be a factor. If it became a problem, the weather was still good behind me. I could circle 180 degrees and return to London or Columbus. Ten minutes later I was slow-flying five feet above the 9,000-foot-long Runway 24, waiting until I was closer to the turnoff near the terminal before setting down. The Cub needs less than 500 feet to land, so touching down at the threshold of a long runway could mean taxiing some distance to get to the tie-down area. Might as well fly.

I tied the Cub down on the ramp next to the

Farm town in Kansas. A town's entire life is spread before you when seen from a small plane.

Hawker-Siddley 125 and went into the terminal to call the Dayton Flight Service Station. They reported that it was all gloom and doom from Dayton through Indiana and looked likely to remain so for another day or two. The system was almost stationary. I grabbed my bags out of the plane, caught a ride into town, and checked in at the Holidome, the closest motel to the airport. It was noon. I had flown a grand total of 200 miles for the day, all in a single leap. At times like this you think seriously about IFR-equipped Bonanzas.

"Is there a bookstore nearby?" I asked the desk clerk.

"A bookstore? Hey, Dianne, is there anyplace that sells books around here?"

"Books?" asked Dianne, who appeared from behind the office partition. "I don't know. Let's

see. I think the Readmore used to have some, but that's pretty far from here."

"How far?" I asked.

"'Bout three miles I guess. Want me to call you a cab?"

"No that's okay, thanks. I'll walk if you'll give me directions."

"You want to walk to Readmore?"

Walking through a town is the best way to get to know it. Springfield, once a bustling industrial town, had fallen on hard times and now seemed to be trying to regain its balance. I walked through a modest residential area, passed the struggling downtown business district, and followed my directions to the small shopping center where the bookstore was located. The name Readmore sounded encouraging; bookstores always hold the promise of new discoveries. Walking past the row of windows in the run-down shopping center, I saw no books. I stepped back into the parking lot in order to see the store names better. There it was, Readmore. I had walked past it. Still I saw no books when I looked through the window. Just rows of potato chips, light groceries, and other convenience goods.

"Do you have any books?" I asked a clerk in the front.

"In the back, by the beer and soda."

Sure enough, there were several racks of paperbacks of all descriptions, with romance novels in command. I browsed, bought a couple of old classics that I had been meaning to read for 30 years, then strolled back through downtown Springfield to a luncheonette and ordered a grilled swiss and tomato.

"I'm sorry, we only have American cheese," the waitress said. No one in the place, including the waitresses, was under sixty-five years old. Everyone else had probably left town when the plants closed.

"American cheese will be fine, thanks. And a Coke, please."

"You said grilled cheese and tomato. Do you mean you want the tomato grilled in with the cheese?" asked the waitress.

"Yes, please."

She walked past the booths to the grill behind the counter to give the order to the cook, then returned.

"The cook says he never heard of grilling the cheese and tomato together. Are you sure that's what you meant?" she said.

"Yes, please. Just put the cheese and tomato together between the pieces of bread, then grill the whole thing."

She smiled. "Okay, sir."

Later, as I was leaving, I saw her pointing me out to the other gray-haired waitress as the fellow who wanted his sandwich that funny way.

It rained most of the next day. I read between phone calls to the Flight Service Station.

Ranch cattle pen.

The weather cleared that night, and I took off early the next morning into a brilliant sky as cheerful as the previous day's had been miserable. I flew for three hours across the farms of Indiana and half way through Illinois before stopping for fuel near Effingham.

With auxiliary tanks full, my Cub carries 60 gallons of fuel and will fly for seven-and-a-half hours at the power settings I use. Six-and-a-half hours is the longest I've ever flown it without stopping, and I almost had to be taken out with a forklift when I landed. Cub seats are not luxurious. Three hours is about right most of the time; long enough to cover some ground, but not so long that I get sore. Even with the auxiliaries only partially filled to save weight, I still have the luxury of plenty of fuel to go further if I wish or to circumnavigate bad weather without having to stop.

VFR navigation in the Midwest is greatly simplified by the north-south, east-west roads that divide the farms. Other than checking the map, the oil pressure and temperature gauges, and your watch now and then, you can spend the whole time admiring the scenery by using the section lines as a compass. There is still a large amount of sparsely settled land in the United States. In fact, with a mindful eye on the aeronautical charts and a detour here and there, it is possible to fly across the whole country without ever seeing a major city, big airport, or entering controlled airspace.

The trend is disappointing, however, for on each trip I see more scars on the earth, less open land, and more controlled airspace. Some of the blight might be termed the price of progress, but too often it is thoughtless, poorly planned, or unnecessary, and driven by greed. I wish more people flew; they could not help but become concerned about the way the rate of change has accelerated in the past few years. You see it all in perspective from the air.

Flying a thousand feet above a small town, one can imagine a whole life cycle from what is seen in a glance. Over there sits the hospital where she was born; there, the house he lived in. Perhaps she worked in a store on the main street, or maybe he farmed on one of the spreads that surround the town. The churches and a school are neatly placed, and on the edge of town is the softball field and cemetery. With the cockpit windows open, you can smell the burning leaves in autumn and the freshly mown fields in summer.

From Effingham I flew west across Indiana and on into Missouri. Along the way I tuned the ADF (Automatic Direction Finder) receiver to local broadcast stations. In addition to music, farm and market reports, and swap-'n-shop programs, there are many call-in shows during the day where listeners telephone the radio host to offer their views on a particular topic. Tuning in as you fly over new towns gives added insight into what the local residents' concerns are, how they think, their taste in music, and what they actually sound like. I almost couldn't believe my earphones when a twist of the dial landed on a discussion of sexual surrogacy. The program's guest, a city slicker from Chicago, was trying to persuade his Show-Me-State listeners that sexual surrogacy was therapy, not prostitution. He was still struggling as I flew out of range.

My first landing in Marshall, Missouri, was 24 years earlier, almost to the day, in an old, ex-Army Super Cub. I had been a student pilot on my first solo cross-country and had had some 21 hours total of flight time. At each stop on a student cross-country, someone has to sign your log book to verify that you actually landed there. A bold, young cropduster named Dyer signed mine in Marshall. He and his boss Sammy were flying Super Cub dusters then, and I never forgot them. I was curious to see if they were still here. On final approach, three hours after departing

Effingham, I could see a couple of ag-planes parked near the airport office. Two older gents came out to look at the Cub and help me refuel when I stopped at the pumps. I asked about my friends.

"No," I was informed, "Sammy died a few years ago, but Dyer the Flyer is still here. Those are his dusters. He just went into town. He'll be sorry he missed you."

There were still a couple of hours left until sunset, and the weather remained brilliantly clear. I wanted to get past Kansas City before stopping for the day and so headed southwest out of Marshall in order to go around the Kansas City TCA to the south and intercept southwest-bound Route 35. Once past the populated areas, I let down to 500 feet above the ground.

The scale is interesting at this height. You are high enough to see terrain features, buildings, or even people in relation to their surroundings, but not so high that you feel detached. You are low enough to feel involved with the land and what is taking place on it. It is the visual equivalent of brushing your fingers against someone's cheek in a caress. Whenever I saw something of particular interest, I slowed down, circled, and photographed it. When you fly higher in a faster plane, you just can't do that, and when it is IFR, forget it. Even if you can see the ground, you can't wander off course to take a look at something or descend to circle and take a few snaps without obtaining a clearance from Air Traffic Control.

From the map Ottawa, Kansas, looked likely for spending the night. The uncontrolled airport had one paved and one grass runway, according to the directory, and motels were not far. I paralleled the highway about a mile to the left, watching the lush textures and colors of the earth in a clear light that was beginning to turn gold. I passed a farmer leading his horse to the barn and another farmer on his tractor. Sometimes people looked up and waved. On another trip,

I had circled a man on his tractor for half an hour taking pictures, moving the airplane to a slightly different position each time like an airborne tripod to get just the right angle. He probably had thought I was lost. I had been—in the beauty of the scene.

I flew with the left window open, left thumb on the map, and marked my position as I moved along. My right hand rested on the stick, moving it a little to the left or right to avoid flying directly over a farm house or a group of cattle standing knee deep in a watering hole in order to keep cool. My feet were on the rudder pedals moving in coordination with the stick. In larger airplanes, flying higher and faster, your feet are usually on the floor unless the air is rough, and you nudge the control wheel once in a while to keep the VOR needle centered or let the autopilot do it for you. But in a small plane, your whole body, as well as eye and mind, are involved with the act of flight, making constant, minute corrections on stick and rudder, even in the smoothest air. It is through this pleasurable, kinesthetic involvement that the airplane becomes an extension of your body and so heightens the experience of flying.

Ottawa Municipal, another small, uncontrolled field, had to be just beyond the next hill. I gave a call on the advisory unicom frequency to announce my position and ask for wind and runway information, but I didn't expect or receive a reply so late in the day. Approaching the gentle up-slope ahead, I added back pressure on the stick. The Cub responded instantly, keeping its set distance above the ground. I added throttle to climb another 500 feet to reach the standard traffic-pattern altitude. The airport was dead ahead, windsock limp. With no wind, any runway would do. I chose the grass one. Landing on grass is much more satisfying than on a hard surface. It has a cushiony feel when the wheels settle into it, and there begins at the same time

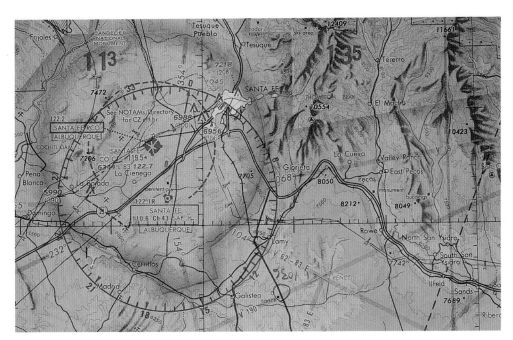

The Santa Fe area as depicted on a sectional chart.

a rumbling sound, increasing as the support of the slowing plane transfers from the wing to the landing gear rolling over undulations of the ground. Tail draggers seem more at home on the grass.

The small airport office was locked, and the airport deserted. I used the outside pay phone to find a room before securing the plane, just in case. The first motel I tried was full, but the second had plenty of rooms, and the owner said he would drive down to the airport and pick me up. By the time he arrived in his van, I had unloaded and tied down. Most airports have tie-down ropes secured on the ramp, but I always carry a set with me. At some of the out-of-the-way places I stop, they come in handy.

The motel was on the outskirts of town, along a road that probably was once the major highway before the four-lane was built and seemed from the older-style architecture to have been constructed some time ago. There was an office and individual rooms strung out in a low row with an empty parking space in front of each door. The owner and his family lived behind the office.

My room was very clean, sparsely furnished with a wood chair, plain table, well-used bed, and lined in dark, simulated-wood panelling. The bathroom fixtures looked older than the TV, which probably was produced about the same time as "Leave It To Beaver."

The young owner and his wife were soft-spoken, rather serious, and very polite when I checked in. From literature in the office and items hanging on the wall, I guessed that they had recently rededicated themselves to the Christian faith.

"Is there a restaurant nearby?" I asked after paying my bill in advance.

"Right down the road about a mile," the man said. "I'd be happy to drive you."

"Thanks, but I've been sitting in the plane 7½ hours today. I can use the walk. Thanks, anyway."

"Well, just call if you want us to pick you up. And in the morning, I'll be happy to take you to the airport before I teach Sunday School. Just stop by about eight."

The restaurant was a roadhouse with one large room, booths, and a juke box and panelled in what looked like the same material as my room. It served beer, steak, and burgers and was filled with animated local folks having Saturday night dinner out.

Later, getting ready for bed that night, I worried about my hosts. The outside of the motel was freshly painted, and they had obviously put in a lot of work to make a go of it, but there was only one car out front. From the air before landing, I had seen the other motel, much newer and nearer the four-lane; that one was full.

I took off the next morning in a sunny but

hazier sky. A phone call to Kansas City Flight Service earlier had indicated that weather would deteriorate as I flew further southwest toward Dalhart in the Texas panhandle. Two hours later, west of Wichita, I started looking at the map for a place to stop and probably stay the night. Wichita Flight Service told me on the radio that there was a line of heavy weather showing up on radar about 50 miles away in southwest Kansas, moving up in advance of another low-pressure center.

When I landed at Pratt, Kansas, 20 minutes later, the visibility was five miles and the ceiling, about 3,000 feet. Still good VFR, but it looked ominously dark to the west and south.

Pratt Airport is partially bordered on two sides by rectangular cattle-feeding pens that are lighted at night and that meet to form a vee. They are, in fact, extensions of former runways. One midnight a couple of years earlier, I had been flying over Pratt in a Bonanza on my way to Dalhart and had looked down in the darkness to see what appeared to be runway lights. They looked strange, though. Three runways of different shapes, all lighted at the same time, aroused my curiosity. I flicked on the map light and pulled out the instrument-approach plate for Pratt. On it was a note that said, "Lighted cattle pens on west side of airport may be mistaken for lighted runways." I had always wondered if anyone had ever landed in one of those cattle pens on a bad night. Now I could ask.

The large, concrete ramp that belonged to the former World War II military field was filled with airplanes of all vintages when I taxied in looking for a place to park. The lady told me on the unicom that today was Annual Pratt Airshow Day. Show time was half an hour from now, and then the field would be closed until it ended. I had to decide whether to refuel quickly and get out before the show in an attempt to press on a few more miles or to stay and chance being

weathered in here. The place was crammed with Pratt residents, as well as scores of fly-in visitors from the region. It looked like fun.

As I was tying down my plane, a vintage Stinson 108 Flying Station Wagon pulled up next to me carrying a couple in their seventies and an elderly poodle. They piled out with their lawn chairs, and we introduced ourselves. They were from a town nearby and had flown together for many years on weekends and vacations to wherever struck their fancies. The old Stinson, for which they paid $2,500 ages ago, was good as new and probably worth $12,000 now. Stinsons are comfortable, perky old birds that fly beautifully, carry four people at a little over 100 miles per hour, and will last longer than the rest of us.

I bought a Pratt Airshow hat and a hot dog from the mobile stand and sat down in a folding chair on the ramp to watch the show. A Stearman was doing an aerobatic routine made doubly exciting by a rapidly approaching thunderstorm from the west. He cut the act short as the rain began, and everyone ducked into the hangar until it passed. When it had, all the fly-in visitors took off to get home before the main weather arrived. Everyone, that is, except a couple of us trying to go southwest. The FBO kindly lent me an old clunker he kept on hand for stranded pilots who needed to drive to the motel. And "No," the gentleman said, no one had ever landed in the cattle pens, quite.

"One night the lights went out on the north-south runway, the only one we keep lighted," he told me. "I was talking on the unicom to a pilot who was coming in, and he said, 'I see the runway lights.' I told him we didn't have any lights on that night, but he would have noticed when he got closer, because the cattle pens are too narrow for a runway.

"Some instructors in the area bring their students here at night under the instrument

A pilot feels very small in a Super Cub over the Grand Canyon.

hood, line them up with the pens, then tell them to take the hood off. It teaches students not to assume anything."

That's a good lesson, I thought. The biggest killer in aviation is complacency.

Pratt is a charming, busy farm community with a movie theater, a couple of family-style restaurants, and a wonderful library. I got to know them all the following day while it rained. The day after, a murder trial, rare in these parts, was due to start. Had the weather remained bad, I had planned to go to the courthouse and listen in, but it was just above minimums as I took off the next morning, and due to improve.

Kansas is monumental in its flatness. I learned to fly here and remember thinking as a student pilot that my engine could quit practically anywhere in the state, and I could just glide straight ahead and find a place to land. Flat country may not sound all that interesting to see from the air, but the farms have a gentle, strong beauty. The view is quite striking when there is nothing but isolated islands of farm houses nestled by protective windbreaks of trees as far as you can see. Each farm has its own signature,

reflecting the personality of its owner.

Kansas is even more provocative than other farm states because it is a land of transition. Flying from east to west across the state, you watch the Midwest end and the West begin. The character of the earth changes from lush farmland to higher, drier plains, as the terrain gradually rises more than 2,000 feet, a fact reflected in the color coding on the sectional chart that turns from light green to tan as altitudes increase.

Flying along Route 54 between Pratt and Liberal to the southwest is a visual treat that sums up Kansas for me. On the map Route 54 forms an elegant curve as it arcs down to the Oklahoma panhandle. Many of the small towns connected by this two-lane ribbon have a set of grain elevators. The tallest structures around, they stand like white sentries visible from miles away. When the weather is clear, you can see as many as three or four elevators ahead, stretching some 20 miles into the distance as you fly from one outpost to the next, past Bucklin toward Kingsdown, Bloom, Minneola, Fowler, Meade, Plains, and Kismet. Each town appears isolated in a powerful, seemingly endless earth ocean that is compassionate in good weather, merciless in bad. Storm systems, especially in winter, howl through here with nothing to stand in the way, nothing except the steadfast grain elevators that anchor memos of humanity to the earth like pushpins.

I mark on the map the exact time that I pass each town so that I can keep track of my ground speed. Fifteen miles in 11 minutes equals 82-miles-per-hour ground speed. With a true airspeed of 105 miles per hour, I have a head-wind component of 23 miles per hour. It will be on my tail going home.

Dalhart is planted in the northwest corner of the Texas panhandle. Seemingly in the middle of nowhere, Dalhart happens to be a conveniently placed refueling spot on the coast-to-coast southern route. With ample runways, a good lunch counter, and an excellent FBO and Flight Service Station all within a few steps of each other, the airport attracts a wide variety of aircraft from crop dusters to jets. Flying people in general are pretty nice folks with a common bond. In the time it takes to refuel and grab a sandwich, it is almost impossible not to meet an interesting fellow pilot in a place like Dalhart.

Super Cubs stir the spirit of adventure in lots of pilots, and at almost every stop, someone comments on the airplane over the radio or after coming by for a look.

"I have one of those back home, and I dearly love it," said a man walking toward me from a Cessna 310. "Where you from?"

"New York," I said.

"You flew all the way from New York in that?" he asked. "That must be great."

"Yeah, it really is fun. Where are you from?"

"Alaska."

"You flew all the way from Alaska in that?" I asked, nodding toward his sleek, twin-engined bomb. "Kind of fast, isn't it?"

"You get so you don't mind it." He intro-duced me to his wife, and we talked airplanes and adventures for a while out on the ramp, then exchanged names and addresses, promising to look each other up if we were ever in New York or Alaska. He took off to the east, and I, to the west. I haven't been to Alaska yet, but I will.

The terrain, still flat, had risen another 2,000 feet between Pratt and Dalhart, and the sectional had turned from light to medium tan. Crossing into New Mexico, it becomes another shade darker. This is where magic land starts.

Kansas was the preparation, northern Texas the initiation, and eastern New Mexico the beginning of my visual voyage through some of the most fascinating terrain in the world that stretches from west Texas westward along the Mexican border to the deserts of eastern California, then northward through Nevada, Utah, and western Colorado. It is, as New Mexico aptly calls itself, a land of enchantment, where sacred Indian grounds, dramatically shaped rock formations, deep gorges, vein-patterned drainage plains, and guarding moun-tains coalesce into a crackling, visible energy. The land, seen through the lens of dry, clear air, is laid bare, allowing the ongoing work of nature's forces to be seen without camouflage. For me, it represents the driving energy of life with the layers of illusion peeled back: vast, powerful, elemental, as beautiful as it is demanding. One can easily imagine that God touched the earth here and said to man, "Be still. Listen. All that you need to know is revealed in this place if you look." It is best seen from the air.

Thoughtfulness is required to fly here, as well as appropriate precautions. There are large, uninhabited areas. If you were forced to land in one with no emergency rations, first-aid kit, clothing for the season, or without notifying someone either by flight plan or word of mouth where you were going and when you were expected back, your options might be

Grand Canyon, south rim.

(Above) Lake Powell on the Arizona-Utah border. (Overleaf, page 193) White Sands National Monument, New Mexico.

severely limited.

It is also important to remember that wings, engines, and pilots need air. The less air there is, the less well planes function, and there is far less air in the higher elevations of the West than there is at sea level. Combined with the higher temperatures of summer, which thins the air even more, the resultant density altitude makes the airplane think it is higher still. Internal combustion engines (basically pumps that generate power by sucking in a load of air, squeezing it, and expanding it rapidly with heat from an explosion) produce less horsepower in thinner air, unless, as in some fancier ships, the air is compressed by a turbocharger to higher density before entering the combustion chambers. Wings produce less lift when the air flowing over them is thinner. The result of less power and less lift is a longer takeoff run and a lower rate of climb. During training, all pilots are taught this and how to figure out the amount of performance that will be lost under specific conditions. It is important to make these calculations and, if necessary, to lighten your load or leave early in the morning when temperatures are cooler.

Flying into New Mexico, still following Route 54, I remember how surprised I was as a student pilot when I opened the throttle for takeoff and it would only go halfway forward. The Super Cub started gathering speed and, still having sufficient power, was content to fly, but everything was taking longer. After attempting to force the throttle forward while trying to keep the ship rolling straight down the runway, I became suspicious and shot a glance at my instructor, Earl Irish, sitting in the rear cockpit, which has its own set of controls linked to those in the front. His hand was clenching his throttle, preventing mine from moving further.

"High-altitude takeoff," he said. "You only have half power."

All of this happened in about three seconds. I completed the takeoff and climbed to altitude, becoming familiar with how the plane performed at half power.

Twenty-five years later, over New Mexico, I recalled that lesson clearly. An awareness of density altitude can mean the difference between flying over the trees at the end of the runway or into them.

The skies ahead were becoming increasingly cluttered with more towering cumulus clouds than normal for a summer afternoon, so I landed at Tucumcari, where there is a Flight Service Station, to check the weather and have a traditional pilot's lunch: Coke and cheese crackers from the vending machine.

"This radar-summary chart doesn't look bad, but its old," the specialist said. "We've had pilot reports of increasing build-ups between here and Santa Fe. There's a low pressure trough aloft that's helping to kick these things up. Otherwise, there's no real weather around. New radar chart will be out in half an hour."

"I'll go have a look and come back if I have to," I said.

"See you later," said the specialist with a knowing smile.

I flew west for another 15 or 20 miles but could tell from my altitude that there was no way of comfortably threading through the build-ups. They were forming in lines. Twenty-five minutes later, I was back at Tucumcari.

"Don't like flying through thunderstorms, eh?" commented the specialist.

Tucumcari is little more than a rest and refueling stop on Route 40 between Albuquerque and Amarillo. There are plenty of gas stations, motels, and friendly people but not much else except wide, open spaces. For one who is dedicated to trying every Mexican eatery in the world, however, the restaurant at the Tucumcari Ramada Inn was an unexpected delight.

The next morning, one hour and 56 minutes after leaving Tucumcari, and eight days after departing East Hampton, I landed at Santa Fe, New Mexico, where I intended to spend a few days. My total flight time so far was 23 hours and 45 minutes, about the same as past westbound trips, but with the unusual number of weather delays, this episode took two days longer than my previous all-time slowpoke record. "Time to spare? Go by air" is the VFR-pilot's motto, at least in most parts of the country.

The Southwest, though, is different. You can count on flying VFR 99 percent of the time. I spent the next 11 days doing just that: first, with Santa Fe as a base, surrounded by a variety of interesting terrain, then at Sedona, Arizona, with its stunning scenery and airport perched atop a flat-topped butte that looked like an aircraft carrier. Each day I made local hops, photographing aerial landscapes that I hoped would show the essence of what captivated me about this part of the world.

One of my favorite areas was northeast of Flagstaff, Arizona, on the western edge of the Painted Desert, which is about a 25-minute flight from Sedona. The drainage patterns, dry gulches, and dormant volcanic domes look like a moonscape. In the slant light of early morning or late afternoon, shapes in the land—practically invisible during the rest of the day—come to life as they are defined by their shadows. One can't observe from the air for long without realizing that the earth is a living creature. It just moves more slowly than we animals.

There is a lonely peace about a small airport like Sedona in early morning. Each day began by arriving at the airport before sunrise to perform the ritual of preflight inspection. Everything was still, and usually I was the only one there, untying the wings and tail from ropes anchored in the ground; making a careful, walk-around inspection to check for signs of leaking oil or fuel;

looking for anything loose, worn, out of place, or missing; draining fuel samples from the tanks and gascolator into a clear cup in order to check for contamination or water that might have condensed in the tank overnight.

From the time of leaving the motel for the pre-dawn drive to the airport, to the moment of climbing into the ship and buckling the harness, I always feel a growing excitement in anticipation of flight. Finally, the moment comes: master switch ON, magneto switch to BOTH, a couple of shots on the primer if it's chilly, pump the throttle, then leave it open a crack, and push the starter button. You can hear the Bendix gear clank into the ring-gear teeth, and the propeller turns—one blade, two blades, three blades—then kicks into a blur. The little airplane trembles as it comes to life, and the morning is still no more, for at this place in a limitless universe, a tiny speck made of steel tubing and aluminum that was formed into a precise shape and covered with cloth is about to fly.

The image of those mornings remains clear in my mind: the clean smells, the quality of light, the sensation of lifting into the air, seeing the runway drop away, and being suddenly alone in another context much vaster than the one now below. Knowing that there will be more of those mornings on future trips fills me with renewed excitement just thinking about it.

On the way back home, I pulled up to the ramp at Columbus, Ohio, to spend my last night on the road. A Lear jet next to me was just lighting the fires. I could hear the growing whine of its turbines over the pocketa-pocketa of my trusty, four-cylinder Lycoming and could see the pilot turn to look at me.

"That's a nice looking Cub," he said over the ground-control frequency.

"Thanks. That's a beautiful machine you've got too," I replied, looking at its sleek shape.

"Yeah, but I'd trade seats with you."

FLYERS HAVE A SENSE
OF ADVENTURES YET TO COME,
INSTEAD OF DIMLY RECALLING
ADVENTURES OF LONG AGO
AS THE ONLY MOMENTS IN WHICH
THEY TRULY LIVED.

—RICHARD BACH

Barnstormer's passenger.

Art director Harvey Stevenson and the author sitting in what used to be the B-25 tail gunner's position. With no glass and a wide field of view, the B-25 offers a superb perch for air-to-air photography.

ABOUT AIR-TO-AIR PHOTOGRAPHY

Air-to-air photography—photographing an aircraft in flight from another aircraft flying in close formation—is a specialized off-shoot from mainstream photography. Composition and lighting are just as critical whether you are shooting a still-life in a studio or in the air. The difference lies in how you control these factors.

In aerial photography the subject airplane flies in formation with the photo plane at exactly the same speed; therefore, both machines must be compatible in performance. The photo-plane pilot maintains the altitude and heading given by the photographer, who usually sits by an open door or window; the subject-airplane pilot flies "on" the photo plane, doing exactly what it does. Executing this safely takes a great deal of skill and training on the part of the subject-airplane's pilot. That's why you see the pilot looking intently at the camera in most pictures.

The photo-plane pilot never looks back at the subject plane. He or she is responsible for spotting other air traffic ahead, handling radio communications, staying out of restricted airspace, and flying smoothly. A word of caution: no matter how terrific a pilot the photographer fancies himself, he must *never* consider flying the photo plane and photographing at the same time. To do so is dangerous and irresponsible.

After a few close calls, I learned early on to fly only with experienced formation pilots. Like instrument flying, formation flying is a skill that must be learned properly and practiced frequently. It is important to know before takeoff who you're flying with.

On one recent photo mission, I was assigned to shoot the TBM 700 prototype, a beautiful, new, single-engine, turboprop business plane. Built by a U.S.-European consortium in Tarbes, France, near the Spanish border, the TBM is a knockout, and I was thrilled to go to Tarbes and photograph it for the TBM Corporation and FLYING magazine.

Our photo plane was a twin-engined Beech Baron 58 that we rented in Paris and flew to Tarbes with pilot Michel Gasc in the left seat. Like the single-engine Bonanza 36, Baron 58s have large double doors in the right rear of the cabin that can be easily (and legally) removed. It gets a little windy and noisy, but the view is great.

Fog and drizzle threatened to delay our shoot, but conditions were good enough for both planes to depart IFR, climb through the cloud deck, and meet at 6,000 feet in sunshine above the overcast. The pilots and I had a thorough pre-flight briefing to discuss altitudes, speeds, camera angles, hand signals, and the radio fix over which we would join up once on top. No eventuality, routine, or emergency was left unconsidered.

At dawn we took off one at a time for proper IFR separation. Within minutes the clouds began to brighten, and we soon broke out into a sparkling clarity of light and air above a billowing sea of white.

Bernard Dorance, TBM's Chief Test Pilot, and Jean Piatek, Flight Test Engineer, were already up in the TBM. Bernard spotted us and quickly brought the TBM to the agreed-upon first position, about 50 feet from our right rear. I asked Marc to continue circling so I could watch the light play on the TBM from different angles. A former fighter pilot, Bernard held position as if he was welded to us by an invisible beam.

With several angles in mind, I told Marc to roll out on a heading of 045 degrees for the first shots. This northeasterly heading would place the sun to the right and forward of us, giving a nice quartering backlight to the TBM 700. With hand signals I motioned Bernard in tight for close-ups; up a little, closer a little, to the rear just slightly, there, that's it.

Motor-drive cameras are convenient in situations like this where you need to shoot quickly. Because of their reliability, quality lenses, and variety of accessories, I have always used Nikon cameras. The lens I use most often is the 105mm, F 2.5, and, second, the 180mm, F 2.8. Longer

This North American B-25 was originally converted to a photo plane by Tallmantz Aviation in California. B-25s gained fame on the Doolittle Tokyo raid on April 18, 1942, and now, 47 years later, they are unsurpassed for photographing high-performance aircraft. Hatches on either side of the fuselage can be opened; there is a big hole at the tail; and on at least two B-25s in the country, the bombardier's greenhouse in the nose has been replaced with low-distortion plexiglass that photographers can shoot through.

telephotos are not only more difficult to hold steady, but they also give a pronounced foreshortening to the perspective that I find unflattering for aircraft. I also use a Kenyon Gyro Stabilizer, a wonderful device that screws into the tripod socket of any camera. It contains battery-driven gyros that help steady the camera in the pitch-and-yaw axis.

Determining the correct exposure for a predominantly white airplane against a white background as we had this day can be tricky, so bracketing exposures is good insurance. You may use three or four times more film, but film is one of the least expensive costs of an assignment.

After half an hour of intensive shooting, the early morning sun over Tarbes began to lose its magic. I had shot several different situations and used up 17 rolls of 36-exposure Kodachrome 25 Professional film, so I waved off the TBM to signal we were through for the day. Each plane secured an IFR clearance for the descent to Tarbes. Back on the ground in the drizzle, we all piled into a car and headed off for breakfast, reliving the flight in animated conversation. Not one of us that morning would have wished to be anywhere else.

Piper Saratoga with left rear passenger and baggage doors removed. Some current single and light twin-engined aircraft are certified for flight with their doors removed and, therefore, make excellent photo ships. Along with the Saratoga series, others include the Piper Seneca, Beech Bonanza 36, and Baron 58.

(Overleaf, pages 196-197) Cessna P210, the Pressurized Centurion.

(Overleaf, pages 198-199) A 1956 Cessna 172. The year 1956 saw Cessna put a nose wheel on the 170 tail dragger and call it the 172. It became the best-selling, four-place airplane in the world, and by the time Cessna suspended production of piston-powered aircraft in 1986, more than 35,000 172s had been sold. The reason for its success was not that it was a spectacular performer in any one category, but that it performed very well in many categories. Simple, safe, easy to fly, and economical, 172s are without question the best all-around, low-cost, four-place airplane our country has produced. The 33-year-old plane flown here by Elliott Ryan and owner Bob Loomis is powered by a 145-h.p. Continental engine and cruises at 104 knots (120 m.p.h.). Later models switched to a 160-h.p. Lycoming, and along with an aerodynamic cleanup over the years, the cruising speed has gone up to 120 knots (138 m.p.h.).

(Overleaf, pages 200-201) North American P-51D Mustang. Deadly in its day 45 years ago, the Mustang still sings the siren's song.

(Overleaf, pages 202-203) Fairchild Swearingen Merlin IIIB. A product of Ed Swearingen's creative mind, the Merlin IIIB offered flying business people an efficient mix of speed, range, and comfort. With two 900-s.h.p. Garrett turboprop engines, the IIIB carried seven passengers at 280 knots (322 m.p.h.).

(Overleaf, pages 204-205) The Piper Malibu provides cabin-class, pressurized comfort with single-engine economy.

Dad. —
I love you very
much. Thanks for
everything you've done.
Love,
Clori
Christmas 89'